P9-APJ-883

150 Ways
to Raise
Creative
Confident
KIDS

150 Ways
to Raise
Creative
Confident
KIDS

SILVANA CLARK

VINE
BOOKS

SERVANT PUBLICATIONS
ANN ARBOR, MICHIGAN

© 1997 by Silvana Clark
All rights reserved.

Vine Books is an imprint of Servant Publications especially designed to serve evangelical Christians.

Published by Servant Publications
P.O. Box 8617
Ann Arbor, Michigan 48107

Cover design: Paul Higdon
Cover photo: © SuperStock. Used by permission.

97 98 99 00 01 10 9 8 7 6 5 4 3 2 1

Printed in the United States of America
ISBN 1-56955-033-6

LIBRARY OF CONGRESS CATALOGING-IN-PUBLICATION DATA

Clark, Silvana.
     150 ways to raise creative, confident kids / Silvana Clark.
        p.   cm.
     ISBN 1-56955-033-6
     1. Child rearing—Unitied States.   2. Creative ability in children—United States.
3. Self-esteem in children—United States.   4. Social skills in children—United States.
I. Title.
HQ769.C612   1998
649'.1—dc21   97-41763
                                                                      CIP

Contents

Activities Using Science, Reading, Treasure Hunts, Bike Rides, and Costumes

Celebrating Your Children With Creativity

Encouraging Creativity While Outdoors

Creative Travel Tips

Creative Culinary Experiences

Creative Games for the Family

Crafts With More Creativity and Fewer Directions

You, Too, Can Raise Inventive, Creative, Exciting People!

How would you answer the following questions?

1. Your daughter wants to construct an apple-picking device to harvest your apples. Would you:
    a. Suggest she get an apple from the refrigerator?
    b. Cut down the apple tree so she'll never get an idea like that again?
    c. Offer to help get the ladder and extra rain gutters from the garage?

2. You and your son are at the store the day after Halloween and see costumes on sale for twenty-five cents each. Would you:
    a. Walk by as you race toward a blue light special on deodorant?
    b. Wonder who in the world would buy Halloween costumes on November 1?
    c. Purchase all the costumes they have for distribution to a children's shelter next year?

If you have chosen "C" as an answer to either of the above questions, congratulations! You're obviously open to discovering new and creative ideas. Now you and your child can set up the rain gutters, pick the apples, and roll them into a basket. Right after Halloween, you and your son can buy all the leftover costumes to give away next year. If you can see an apple-picking machine in rain gutters and a way to make some kids happy through the purchase of leftover costumes and can share those experiences with your own children, you're on your way to raising creative and confident kids.

Albert Szent-Cyörgyi, the Nobel Prize physician, stated, "Discovery consists of looking at the same thing as everyone else and thinking something different." We have all heard of people with strong creative abilities. These are the people who can see a "pet" in a rock or a "hula" in an ordinary plastic hoop. These are the people who leave the rest of us scratching our heads and saying, "Why didn't I think of that?" Perhaps this kind of creativity is the result of learning to "think something different" about the most ordinary of items.

This book is about looking at life and family activities with new eyesight. It's about doing more than spending an hour or two playing a game of Monopoly with your kids and calling it "quality family time." It's about exposing your children to the wonders of God's world. It's about thinking of fifty uses for a spoon. It's about being willing to get glue on the table or dirt on the floor to create an art project or a dish garden. It's about staying home from work some day and using the time to build the world's-greatest-ever super fort with your son.

We all believe that we are made in the image of a creative God. Because we believe this, doesn't it stand to reason that we should be able to lay claim to a tiny bit of God's creativity for our children and for ourselves? But to know how to access his creativity, we have to learn to pay attention to what he's made and given to us. Aardvarks and zebras, gravity and zero gravity, salt water and fresh water, tall

Mount Everest and the deep Grand Canyon, speedy jaguars and sluggish sloths. We have to learn to watch and listen for his creative inspiration.

We are born with a curiosity that provokes creativity. Young children love to explore and discover. They're fascinated with the way the wheels on their strollers rotate. They can become totally engrossed in the way a dandelion sprouts from the soil. But too often when they put their hands on the wheels of the stroller to see how they turn or pull up the dandelion to see its roots, well-meaning parents stop them because they might get a little dirt on themselves. It's as though clean hands and clean clothes were more important than the great adventure of learning hands-on. We don't even realize we've just stifled their sense of discovery and creativity.

It's not enough to tell our children to "be creative." They need examples, tools, and an environment conducive to creative thought. Encouraging creativity in children means setting an example for them. They need to see us being creative. I'll never forget the look on my daughter's face when she came home from a post-Halloween shopping trip with her dad. "Mom, you'll never believe what we did!" The words bubbled out. "Dad and I bought thirty-four Halloween costumes. Thirty-four!" So we did what I recommended above, and the next fall we challenged Trina to think of creative ways to disburse the costumes. Her very creative idea was to distribute them to a group home for young children and a shelter for battered women and their children. Dad had led the way to creativity.

Business leaders are lamenting the lack of creativity in our young people today. Employees come to work, do their jobs the way they've always done their jobs, and rarely, if ever, have a new or innovative idea about how to "build a better mousetrap." It starts in school when the children's creativity is limited to bringing the latest action figure or fashion doll to show-and-tell time. None of them are nearly as creative as the little boy in the TV advertisement who is told to bring something soft to school, and he brings toilet paper.

Creativity adds flavor to our lives. It reduces the boredom and routine we often find ourselves experiencing. Young stay-at-home moms with small children are often victims of boredom when they don't need to be. Think creatively about even the smallest, most mundane routines of life. Do things like taking your kids to the mall before it opens and letting them join the mall walkers strolling up and down. It's a creative way to break their routine, and in the process, all of you will get some exercise. Hey, they might even be ready for a nap when they get home! Do things like taking a long, hard look at their toys—with them—helping them decide what they are truly using and what some other child might be able to use. Keep the toys that stimulate creativity. Get rid of those that don't.

If the boredom is getting you and the kids down, stop whining and do something about it. Several years ago, I decided to do something about my routine, mundane life. I decided to fulfill a lifelong dream to train a dog for television commercials. At the time, I had an eight-week-old springer spaniel puppy named Sherman. Since I couldn't find any guidelines on "How to Make Your Dog Rich and Famous in Ten Easy Steps," I had to be creative and develop my own plan. I started by taking Sherman to perform at schools and churches. It built up his experience. Then I contacted producers and directors and submitted a resume and an eight-by-ten glossy photo of Sherman. It wasn't long until Sherman began receiving attention from key people in the film industry. Since that time he's been on billboards, "modeled" for catalogs, and filmed commercials for Honda, Chrysler, Red Devil Paint, Reebok, and many others.

Sherman's career also opened a career for Trina, my oldest

daughter. She often went along to assist with Sherman during a photo shoot. Seeing her, several directors decided to cast her for commercials. Later, when my second daughter, Sondra, was old enough, she became involved as well. Today, at seven, she's done stage performances around the country as well as commercials for Mattel, Fisher Price, Playskool, and many others. We weren't looking for careers for the girls, but that's the beauty of creativity—you never know where it's going to take you. You never know what new experiences creativity will bring to your life.

Creativity is fun! Ben and Jerry, of ice cream fame, were bored to death with vanilla and chocolate ice cream. So they set out on a creative flavor adventure that led to such mouth-watering flavors as Chocolate Chip Cookie Dough, Rain Forest Crunch, and Wavy Gravy. Which ice cream sounds like more fun to you—vanilla or Cherry Garcia?

Creativity can help children make positive decisions about their lives. If your child knows home is a fun and safe place, they'll want to invite friends over. As they make caramel apples, build a fort out of refrigerator boxes, or have a Rollerblade derby, children gain a sense that creativity is encouraged. They learn to put dreams into action and risk new ideas. They'll feel good about themselves, and when peer pressure tries to sway them toward negative experiences like involvement with gangs and drugs, they will not need those activities to give them a sense of self-worth.

Creativity doesn't have to drain the checkbook. While there are some expenses, they can be minimal. One of our favorite family activities is simply playing hide-and-seek in the house. Our daughters plan in advance where to hide by setting up pillows or boxes to "casually" disguise their hiding spot. Once, they went so far as to empty out the fifty-pound dog food bag so Trina could hide inside.

It was a great idea, but our St. Bernard gave away her hiding spot by barking and laying on top of his beloved dog food bag. Trina's cries for help brought us running to save her from being crushed by our 180-pound pet! We add more fun to hide-and-seek by trying to get the hidden people to laugh. My husband will go into a room where one of us is hiding and tell silly jokes, make disgusting noises, or just say, "Is that giggling I hear?" We cover our mouths, trying not to make any noise, but sooner or later we break down and laugh out loud.

This book has been written to spark new ideas and to produce many hours of creative fun with your family. Are you ready for the great adventure? All right. Let's begin!

Activities Using Science, Reading, Treasure Hunts, Bike Rides, *and* Costumes

Creativity Counts

A recent study asked one hundred CEOs of Fortune 500 companies, "What traits do you see as being important for business success?" The number one answer was, "Creativity." Intelligence was number two. Let's face it. Not all of us have IQs that qualify us to join Mensa.* We can, however, all be creative in our own way.

We need to set the stage to develop children with the skill to think creatively. Creativity is more than developing an item like the pet rock or hula hoop. It's asking yourself and your children, "Is there another way to do this?" When we look at Jesus' life, we see that over and over he used nontraditional thinking. He never once said, "That's how everyone else is doing it." Think about some things you do every day. Is there a creative way to approach them that would bring new meaning and insight?

Ideas for a Creative Life

- Do you always say grace before meals? How about praying *after* the meal is over? Try singing a hymn in the middle of the meal. One family really turned things upside down by thanking God for the fresh blackberry pie and then eating dessert first!

---

*Mensa is an organization for highly intelligent people. Just in case you want to know if you qualify for Mensa (only 2 percent of the population does), ask for their application test: 1-718-934-3700. Who knows, there may be a genius in your family!

- When a child comes to you with a problem, ask: "What is the easy way to take care of the situation?" Then ask, "What is an unusual or unique way to work out this problem?"
- Encourage children to express their views, even when they are young. This helps them feel free to develop new ideas.
- Show children they have options in life. Creative people are known for looking at numerous possibilities in any situation.

That Extra Effort

Raising creative and adventurous children is more labor-intensive than raising couch potatoes. At the end of the day, think how easy it is to plop in front of the television set and mindlessly watch whatever pops up on the screen. "I'm tired," you tell yourself. "I deserve to relax." In the Gospels, numerous instances show Jesus got tired, both physically and mentally. On several occasions the Bible tells us so many people were around him he had no chance to eat. Yet he gave that extra effort and took time to think about other people and their needs.

Your children don't need you to be a martyr who spends every waking moment fulfilling all their desires. They do need someone to set an example of how to use available resources to lead a productive life.

Ideas for a Creative Life

- Tired after work? Get a stopwatch, gather the family, and see how far you can *walk* in seven-and-a-half minutes. At the seven-and-a-half-minute mark, turn around and walk home. The next day, try to speed up the pace and walk further. Within fifteen minutes, your family has: been together, exercised, and you probably all feel more refreshed than before the walk.

- Stop at a craft store and get a packaged kit of origami papers. The kits come with patterns, so everyone can fold and create his or her favorite design. Your ten year old isn't going to announce, "Guess what, Mom? I bought some origami paper with my allowance, so we can have a family activity." The extra step of obtaining supplies and ideas begins with adults.

- Borrow flannel board stories from a Sunday school teacher. At bedtime, instead of reading a book, use the flannel figures to enrich the Bible story. One family enjoyed using Dad's chest and stomach as the flannel board!

"Children are a great deal more apt to follow your lead than to go the way you point."
Author unknown

Finding the Fun Factor

As parents, we select baby-sitters with care, keep our child's immunizations up to date, and provide a safe home environment. But what about the Fun Factor? The American Institute for Stress reports 70 percent of Americans suffer from a high level of stress at least once a week. Humor is one way to reduce tension. When it comes to disciplining children, a lighthearted touch often prevents major outbreaks of frustration.

One evening our normally cooperative four year old announced,

"I'm not tired and I don't want to put on my nightgown!" Allan sim- ply went to her dresser and pulled out three nightgowns and two sets of pajamas. Without saying a word, he placed the items on the floor in a large circle. Sondra watched, not sure if this was a ploy to get her to bed immediately. Instead her dad asked, "Remember when we went on the cake walk at the school carnival? This is a pa- jama walk. I'll play music and you walk on each item. When the music stops, that's what you get to wear to bed. We'll practice a few times, of course." Suddenly, a potentially negative situation became a fun event as Sondra jumped from item to item with Sousa marches in the background. She ended up in bed, smiling and con- tent with the feeling that the world is a safe and fun place.

As we teach our children about God, they need a reference point, usually their own father. If Dad is always yelling and too busy to play, how can they understand the concept of a loving, caring God? The next time you feel anger toward your child:

- Count to ten or one hundred before speaking. (It's an old stand- by that works.)
- Put *yourself* in time-out—leave the room until you calm down.
- Ask yourself, "How serious is this situation? Will I laugh about it in two years?"

Subscribe to *The Joyful Noiseletter,* by The Fellowship of Merry Christians, 1-800-877-2757. Also see *Keeping Your Family Together When the World Is Falling Apart* by Dr. Kevin Leman, Focus on the Family Books.

Tacky Tourists and Hillbillies

Everyone loves a birthday party, but what about those times when you feel like having a party just to get together with friends? Parties centered around a basic theme give you a focus for food, decorations, and even costumes. Rather than simply saying, "Come on over after church," get the creative juices flowing and invite people over for a Tacky Tourist Party or an Arts and Crafts Extravaganza. Children can participate by decorating and providing input on the menu. A theme is a great icebreaker when inviting new people to your regular circle of friends.

Ideas for a Creative Life

- For the Tacky Tourist party, simply tell people they need to dress as the stereotypical tourist in Bermuda shorts, plaid shirt, and loafers with black socks. Ask a travel agent for posters, prepare an assortment of ethnic foods, and you are all set. Be sure to take photos, especially if your pastor attends wearing his Hawaiian shirt and checkered pants.
- Children enjoy a Hillbilly Party. Invite them to come wearing old clothes and then eat without silverware. Have everyone participate in a jug band using spoons, combs, washboards, and overturned buckets.
- Bible Parties encourage people to get out the bathrobes and dress like their favorite Bible character. One family served pita bread to represent manna and had everyone create a sandwich from an assortment of fillings.
- Feeling buggy? Invite friends for a bug party. As they arrive, distribute pipe cleaner antennae attached to plastic headbands.

String yarn around the living room to create a giant spider web. Have a bug piñata filled with gummy worms.

- Don't forget the ever-popular 1950s parties with poodle skirts and slicked-back hair. Serve root beer floats and enjoy an old-fashioned taffy pull.

> Book: *Pick-a-Party: The Big Book of Party Themes* by Patty Sachs, Meadowbrook Press. Note: If you have a question about theme parties, Patty Sachs will answer you through e-mail. Contact her at partysachs.internetmci.com.

Sweaty at Church

Many day-to-day experiences can easily become creative experiences. Jesus preached from a boat instead of standing behind a wooden pulpit. He taught with dramatic parables rather than reading from a book. He even walked on water. While most of us only mop up spilled water, we can look for ways to take an ordinary situation and add an original aspect.

When baking bread for a company dinner and the dough fails to rise, do you moan about your shortcomings as a cook? Or do you hand your guests a chunk of dough and tell them to shape their own pretzels for appetizers? When a family discovered their car wouldn't start one Sunday morning, the parents suggested riding their bikes to church. Granted, they arrived a few minutes late and a bit sweaty, but the children saw how a problem can be solved by looking for alternative answers. They had such an enjoyable time riding bikes, they now allow extra time and ride to church on a regular basis.

Ideas for a Creative Life

- Even the way in which you assign mundane chores can take on a new twist.

  List all the jobs that need to be done on small strips of paper.

  Insert one piece of paper into each of several balloons and inflate them. (Balloons can be color-coded according to the complexity of the task so the children can choose.)

  Everyone races to sit on two balloons and pop them. Half the fun is trying to pop the balloon as it scoots out from under you. When the balloon pops, read the strip of paper to find out your assigned job.

  The children will begin their jobs in a better frame of mind than if simply told: "Josh, vacuum the car," and, "Emily, clean the dog kennel."

Check out a web page devoted to creativity quotes at www.bemorecreative.com.

The M & M Experience

Have you ever attended a concert of senior citizens playing harmonicas? Visited a church with a different style of worship? Eaten a breakfast sponsored by a rural grange? These are just a few activities available when your family goes on an "M & M" or "Memory-Making" Experience.

The Memory-Making Experience involves an element of mystery and surprise for everyone. The premise is simple: a designated person is responsible for providing the family with a new experience they have not had before. A Memory-Making Experience follows three simple rules:

1. No complaining about the event. The goal is to experience something new, even if it is out of your comfort zone.
2. It must be free or low cost.
3. The activity must be something the majority of family members have never done before.

Ideas for a Creative Life

We've all heard about events such as a Highland Dance Contest or a track meet for Special Olympic Athletes, but do we go? One family plans a monthly M & M Experience with their two teenagers taking an active part in planning the event. The fifteen-year-old movie buff told the family his experience would take them back to an era before cars were commonplace. The family then walked two miles to a local theater to watch a rare 1920s silent film, complete with a lively piano player. Other families have attended the dedication of a new fire station, watched a Mexican Hairless Dog Show on TV, and volunteered to judge a costume contest at the local Senior Center. The experience of participating in a new activity as a family is sure to provide a feeling of closeness as well as a few laughs.

Almost every newspaper carries a section called "Upcoming Events." Look over the activities and call the contact number. You'll be surprised at the number of informative activities taking place in your community.

Beyond Groundhog Day

Everyone celebrates traditional holidays, so how about adding fun to an otherwise dull week by celebrating an untraditional holiday? What are you doing June 6? Since that is National Yo-Yo Day, have a new yo-yo at everyone's place at dinner. An ordinary meal becomes a laughter-filled event as people try to demonstrate their favorite yo-yo techniques. One family, who knew their pastor and his wife enjoyed coffee, invited them for a gourmet coffee-tasting party. The occasion? National Gourmet Coffee Day on September 16, of course!

By celebrating ordinary days with a special meal or activity, you demonstrate to children the joy of everyday living. It is all too easy to say, "I hate Mondays; I just can't seem to get going," or "January is such a bleak month. I have the mid-winter blues." We have the power to make our lives interesting if we make the effort to create new experiences for our families. Granted, celebrating "Sneak Zucchini Onto Your Neighbor's Porch Night" on August 8 will not solve the world's problems, but it will put fun into your own life.

One family got into the spirit of unusual holidays by celebrating National Twinkies Day on April 6. Several families got together to enjoy an evening of games such as: soccer in the garage using a Twinkie for a ball, Twinkie Toss into a garbage can, and a Twinkie treasure hunt. For refreshment, everyone enjoyed milk and Twinkies, of course!

Ideas for a Creative Life

- Mix up dough to celebrate National Homemade Bread Dough Day on November 17. Let everyone shape an individual loaf.
- Invite friends over for Creative Flavor Ice Cream Day on July 20. Put out vanilla ice cream to combine with fruit, spices, flavorings, and anything else that is creative yet edible.
- Celebrate "Read-a-New-Book Month" in December by reading a variety of books that celebrate the true meaning of Christmas.

> You'll enjoy this book listing 3,000 holidays:
> *Celebrate Today* by John Kremer.
> Phone: (515) 472-6130. Open Horizons Press.

Unexpected Treasures

Think back to some memorable gifts you've received. Maybe you were fortunate to get the horse you wanted for your tenth birthday, but in most cases small unexpected gifts are the most special.

Gifts of time and experiences also produce positive memories. One teenager told a friend, "My dad's kind of old-fashioned, but I remember how he would play Crazy Eights with me night after night. It was my favorite game when I was little, and he never complained about being too bored or too busy."

Proverbs 3:27 says, "Do not withhold good from those to whom it is due, when it is in your power to do it." Often, when I think I "should" call a sick friend, or "should" write a note to a shut-in, that verse prompts me to action. It is within my power to "do good" the majority of the time. How do you do good in providing physical and emotional gifts to your family?

Give unexpected hugs, even to reluctant teens.

Prepare a family member's favorite meal for no reason other than to make him or her feel special.

Listen without making suggestions or "constructive" comments when children talk to you. (This also works well with your spouse.)

Say "thank you!" when family members remember to turn out lights, share toys, or replace the empty toilet paper roll.

Ideas for a Creative Life

One evening my husband and daughter read *The Philharmonic Gets Dressed*. The book described the various ways orchestra members dressed and arrived for their concert. The last page stated: "They are the members of the Philharmonic Orchestra, and their work is to play." At that point, my husband secretly pushed the remote control on the tape recorder to fill the room with the sounds of the New York Philharmonic Orchestra. The wonder in Sondra's face convinced me he had just created a memory. He used the concept of "not withholding good" to add an element of fun to reading a book.

Book: *The Philharmonic Gets Dressed*, Karla Kuskin,
New York: Harper Trophy, 1982.

Fun and Fitness

If yours is like most families, exercise is a low priority, even though we know it is beneficial. As parents, we watch our children's soccer and baseball games but have little time or inclination to play ourselves. With some planning, even family fitness can be enjoyable and worthwhile.

Ideas for a Creative Life

If your family has never exercised together, begin by taking a simple walk. At each corner, flip a coin. Heads ... turn right. Tails ... turn left.

- A family with two preschoolers had a ritual of producing their own mini-parade each evening. Dad pulled the two year old in a balloon-decorated stroller. The neighbors clapped and waved as the parade walked by. Another father brought smiles to whomever saw him pushing his daughter in a wheelbarrow on their evening walks.

- To provide some fun, divide your family into two groups and let each group produce its own exercise routine on video. Then when the family needs to get moving, pop in the tape and watch your own production of "The [your family's name] Exercise Tape." Watching a mom lead her version of step-aerobics with a toddler helping her by moving her plastic steps is guaranteed to exercise your funny bone.

- Check local recreation departments to see about drop-in basketball or All-Comers Track Meets, where your family can exercise together.

- Look for times to get in extra walking. Park the car at the far end of the church parking lot. One family got quick exercise by walking at a rapid pace around their house ten times. Half the family went one direction and the other half the opposite way. They thought up funny greetings to say whenever they passed each other.

- Incorporate movement into daily routines. If you take the bus to work, get off a few stops early and walk the rest of the way. Let your children see you as a moving target rather than a lethargic couch potato.

Going to watch TV tonight? Make a rule that as soon as a commercial comes on, everyone has to jump, dance, and move until the program resumes.

Getting Use Out of Your Garage Door

In order to raise adventurous children, parents need to expose them to thinking beyond traditional ideas. It is all too easy to take the simple way out and think the way everyone else does. Do you always take the same dish to potlucks? See what happens when you pick up a pizza on the way to your next potluck. If you don't think you are a creature of habit, try moving your kitchen wastebasket six inches. You'll immediately notice the difference. At least once a day ask yourself, "How can I adapt or change what I'm doing?" It is an easy way to stimulate your own creative thinking so that you can stimulate your children's creativity.

Ideas for a Creative Life

If Grandma's flying in for a visit or your college-age son is coming home for break, go beyond putting balloons on the front door. How about creating a huge greeting card?

Using butcher paper or newsprint, draw a four- to six-foot greeting card. Attach it to the inside to the bottom of your closed garage door. As the honored guest pulls into the driveway, push the button to open the garage door. Your giant card will unfurl slowly. Add balloons and streamers for additional special effects.

One family traced themselves on newsprint, cut out their body shapes, and attached them to the garage door. When Grandma arrived, life-sized paper family members greeted her. She felt honored by the special sign, and children saw once again how to use nontraditional thinking. It's now become a family tradition to have a "Garage Door Card" for all special occasions. An added benefit is that even young children can participate by taping streamers to the door while older children make the cutouts or drawings.

Making the extra effort to produce a giant greeting card shows children another way to express love. They quickly see the honored guest's face light up in surprise at seeing a six-foot card unfurling when the garage door is opening.

Teaching Creative Behavior by Doris Shallcross, Bearly Ltd.

Back to Basics Week

Raising creative and caring children is not always an easy process. Sometimes valuable lessons are learned through serious undertakings. To help children gain an understanding of people less fortunate than themselves, many families establish a Back to Basics Week. This is simply a time for families to understand what they need, not what they want.

"Whenever my kids start taking things for granted and asking for the latest in clothes and toys, we scale back for a week," says a mother of three. Back to Basics Week is not a punishment but a gentle way to experience a modified lifestyle. Everything is scaled back. Dad gives up espresso and the kids give up candy at the neighborhood grocery store. Mom serves low-cost, nutritious meals minus dessert and even the dog gives up treats. During this week there are no rented videos or trips to fast food restaurants. Some families even walk or use public transportation. Even brown bag lunches are simplified without the usual extra treats. This is a good time for the family to learn the difference in cost between food prepared from scratch and convenience foods. Have the children compare the price of pre-cut stir-fry vegetables and salads to vegetables they cut up themselves.

Ideas for a Creative Life

If you decide to conduct a Back to Basics Week:
- Discuss with children why you are scaling back. Hopefully the experience gives children a greater understanding for other people who have fewer worldly goods.

- Ask children for their own ideas on how to cut back for the week.
- Check out library books depicting stories about low-income families. Emphasize how family relationships are more important than material possessions. The book *Material World: A Global Family Portrait,* by Peter Menzel (Sierra Press), depicts in graphic photographs families around the world with everything they own.
- Back to Basics Week is not as exciting as a trip to an amusement park; yet the lessons learned make a lasting impression.

Frugal Finances is a newsletter written by a Christian stay-at-home mom. For a free sample, send a self-addressed stamped envelope to: Kristin Fruhwirth, Box 243, Grayslake, IL 60030.

Just Singin' in the Rain

L iving in Washington state gives us plenty of opportunity to learn how to adjust activities to the weather. We believe in getting full use of our raincoats and plastic boots. If you've planned to take a walk after dinner and it begins to rain, show the children how to make the best of the situation by walking under umbrellas, arm-in-arm, while belting out "Singin' in the Rain" and "Raindrops Keep Fallin' on My Head."

Rainy days are wonderful for being cozy with hot chocolate and a good book. However, four or five days of nonstop rain can produce severe cases of cabin fever. One family has a tradition that when it rains more than three days in a row, they put on rain gear and walk the one and a half miles to the local convenience store. There, everyone gets seventy-five cents to spend. Upon arriving at home, all the treats are spread out and shared. This year their six-month-old baby participated with her own rain-proof canopy over her in the backpack. (She didn't get seventy-five cents to spend, though.)

Ideas for a Creative Life

- Borrow a microscope, and collect rainwater samples. Discuss bacteria, pollution, and water conservation.
- Set out a can and measure the daily rainfall. Compare your results with the local meteorologist's report.
- Put on boots and splash in the mud. Yes, you'll be wet and dirty, but isn't it something you've always wanted to do? Think of the memories you are creating.
- Go to a park in the rain. Get on a swing and pump as high as you can. Swinging high while rain pelts your face is certainly not an everyday situation.
- Sprinkle dried tempera paint on paper. Take your paper out into the rain. Watch as the rain creates "splash paintings."
- Instead of complaining about the rain, use it as an opportunity to have fun. One family looked so happy walking around their neighborhood in the rain, two other families quickly dressed in rain gear and joined them. Fourteen people created a colorful parade with umbrellas, boots, and rain hats.

Go ahead and ignore your mother's advice. You <u>won't</u> catch a cold if your feet get wet!

Rocking and Splashing

A s any parent knows, actions speak louder than words. We constantly tell our children to be more creative and think for themselves, while at the same time we encourage conformity. Can't you still hear your parents saying, "If everyone jumped off a bridge, would you jump too?"

Ideas for a Creative Life

- Let your children see you in action as you attempt a new skill or expand your own creative thinking. My husband Allan makes a point of doing something unusual when he teaches children's worship time. As a role model, he wants to show that Bible stories are exciting and pertinent to the lives of five and six year olds.

- When telling the story of Jesus sleeping in the boat during a big storm, Allan lugged our sixteen-foot canoe into the classroom. One child was designated to be Jesus. He pretended to sleep as the other children were disciples in the boat. As the "storm" approached, Allan rocked the canoe and gently splashed warm water on the disciples. Only when Jesus awoke and told the seas to be still did the rocking and splashing stop.

- During a lesson on Jonah and the big fish, Allan draped a parachute over tables and chairs (you could use a tarp or a tablecloth). The children crawled inside the "fish" to hear the story and practice their memory verse. The hot and crowded feeling under the parachute gave the class a firsthand experience about Jonah's discomfort.

  Research shows people learn only 10 percent of what they hear or see, but they learn 90 percent of what they directly experience. It's all right if children question their faith. To encourage healthy questions about Christianity, they need to feel, touch, and even get splashed in a boat. Yes, it requires extra preparation time to create a giant fish in a crowded Sunday school. However, such preparation demonstrates creativity and caring. If you don't teach Sunday school on a regular basis, ask if you can visit a class as an "enrichment" person. Bring in an appropriate object lesson, dress up as a Bible character, or drag in a canoe!

> "Kids learn a lot about getting to the moon, but very little about getting to heaven."
>
> David Jeremiah

Oh, Those Adoring Fans!

Most of us, at one time or another, have wondered what it would be like to be famous. How does Amy Grant feel as she rides in a limousine and is greeted by adoring fans everywhere she goes? How could you lack self-esteem if people were always clamoring for your autograph? Consider giving someone the chance to be "famous" for a birthday or another special event.

In Hollywood there is an actual business called "Rent a Fan Club" which provides pretend "fans" to greet a person with screams, flash pictures, and requests for autographs.

On a smaller and cheaper scale, organize a special instant celebrity service for your sixteen year old's birthday or your parents' anniversary. After hearing their pastor state that while his life was fulfilling to him, it was not very exciting, one church decided to make him a celebrity. They arranged for a board member to meet the pastor for lunch at an upscale restaurant. As the pastor and his wife unsuspectingly parked their car and walked toward the restaurant entrance, they were mobbed by thirty-five members of the congregation yelling: "There he is!" "Oh, I can't believe it's him!" People wearing fake press badges with fancy cameras snapped flash pictures while others swooned and screamed, begging for autographs. Secret servicemen in suits and dark glasses surveyed the crowd. Several "bodyguards" protected the pastor from his adoring fans. Needless to say, he received top-notch service that day. After that he also became more careful about what he said in his sermons!

Ideas for a Creative Life

You don't need to go to the extent this congregation did to make someone feel special, but you could:

- Pat your child's shoulder as he or she walks by.
- If your child normally takes the bus or walks home from school, surprise the child by picking him or her up at school. (Teens act embarrassed but usually like getting a ride home.)
- Say something complimentary about your child to another adult and let your child hear it too.

The next time your child walks into the room, stand up and give him or her a rousing standing ovation. You applaud at outstanding theatrical performances, so applaud because you have an outstanding child.

Silly, Yet Sensible

Sometimes asking a silly question triggers creative thinking. Every Thursday, a family with two teenagers assigned a family member to come to dinner prepared with a thought–provoking question or an unusual item. One of the items brought to the table was a fluorescent yellow meat tenderizer—the kind you pound—with a flamingo head for a handle. When the item was shown, family members made serious (and not-so-serious) attempts to guess what it was. Finally they had to be told. Another time they asked questions such as: "How would our lives be different if we had eight fingers on each hand?" "What if we didn't have designated lanes in which to drive cars?" The questions encourage expanded thinking. The answers ranged from thoughtful to hilarious.

On the surface, these questions seemed humorous, but more and more businesses find humor increases productivity. Many of the workshops I do center around ways to develop humor in the workplace. Give your children a head start in the business world by asking silly questions at home. Not only do they have fun, but you get their creative juices flowing and you convey that life is good. At school, children learn about AIDS, gangs, and being cautious around strangers. One seventh grader told his teacher, "I wish I could just have time to do something fun. I'm busy with homework, selling candy for the soccer team, and helping my mom with our new baby. Why can't I just laugh and have fun?" Children need time to be children.

Ideas for a Creative Life

Next time you talk with your child, instead of asking, "How was school?" ask:

- "What would school be like if only eight year olds were allowed to be teachers?"
- "What are ten things you can do with a pair of suspenders?"
- "When would it be a good idea to wear shoes over your ears?"

> If you are brave enough, let your children play "Stump the Parent." They get to ask *you* questions ranging from "What is heaven like?" to "Why can't we flap our arms and fly?"

Lights! Camera! Action!

Family talent shows provide entertainment unrivaled by any Broadway production. (Especially if proud relatives are in the audience.) Even a three year old can give a rousing rendition of "Twinkle, Twinkle, Little Star." Adults can lip-sync their favorite oldies tune while teens play in an air band. Or get creative and showcase other kinds of talents. Have Dad show how to change spark plugs or Junior share his extensive bottle cap collection.

A family with four children planned a yearly magic show for close friends. David Copperfield certainly had nothing to worry about in terms of competition; but some of the tricks were impressive enough to prompt cries of "How did you do that?"

A college student fondly recalls the talent shows their family held on a regular basis. "I remember being ten years old and crying because I wasn't selected for the role of Clara in my ballet class production of "The Nutcracker." My dad bought me a new pink tutu, planned a talent show, and had me dance the role of Clara for our family. He danced with me as the prince, even though he never had a ballet lesson in his life! I'll never forget the experience."

Talent shows not only provide an opportunity to gain confidence in performing before an audience, they are also a fun place to see adults play their dusty violins, blow into a harmonica, or attempt a headstand.

Studies show the number one fear of Americans is speaking before a group of people; yet, over and over we hear how schools and businesses stress the importance of communication skills. Your family talent show may be lacking in professional talent, but it is providing your children with opportunities to build confidence and composure before a group. Applause and a standing ovation tell a child, "I did it! I can perform in front of a group!"

Ideas for a Creative Life

Talent Show Possibilities:
- acrobatics
- soccer techniques
- cooking demonstrations
- dancing
- singing—try a quartet, lip-syncing
- knitting or magic demonstrations

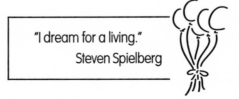

"I dream for a living."
Steven Spielberg

Captain Hook and Peter Pan

"**M**ommy, I don't want you to leave," wailed my three-year-old daughter. Naturally I felt guilty, even though I work out of my home and am gone only two or three days a month.

My husband, whom you've already discovered has a flair for creative thinking, disappeared with Sondra into a closet from which I soon heard whispering and muffled giggles. Within minutes they came out and Sondra said with a smirk, "Have fun, Mom. I'll see you later."

Driving to the airport, neither one would tell me why they were both so cheerful. I kissed them good-bye, went to a speaking engagement, and flew home. When I got off the airplane I was shocked to see my husband and daughter dressed in costumes from Peter Pan. Allan had made Sondra a green felt tunic, a pixie hat complete with a peacock feather, and pixie shoes with upturned toes. He was dressed as Captain Hook in an old black cape, tights, and instead of a "hook" for his false hand, he used the prongs of a fork. Since that time it has become a tradition for them to dress up in costume when they pick me up at the airport. So far I have been greeted by:

- Annie and Daddy Warbucks (They actually put a temporary red dye in Sondra's blonde hair.)
- The Phantom of the Opera and Christina
- Two secret service agents, complete with black glasses and walkie talkies.
- 1950s characters with poodle skirts and slicked back hair.
- Dorothy and the Scarecrow from *The Wizard of Oz.*

Now when I announce I'm leaving, Sondra and Allan begin planning their next costume extravaganza. Using creativity, Allan took a potentially negative situation and turned it into a positive experience. He *has,* however, encouraged me to take a taxi home occasionally … so he doesn't have to continue to make a spectacle of himself at the airport!

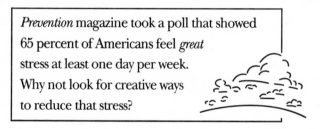

Prevention magazine took a poll that showed 65 percent of Americans feel *great* stress at least one day per week. Why not look for creative ways to reduce that stress?

Creative Dating

In striving to provide quality time for our children, adults often overlook their own relationships with a spouse and adult friends. Spending time discussing topics beyond knock-knock jokes enriches our lives, which in turn enriches our children's lives. It's all too easy to get in a rut of only engaging in brief snippets of conversation with adults.

Ideas for a Creative Life

Children benefit from seeing their parents interact with other adults. Putting thought into these experiences shows children creativity continues throughout life.

Here are some ideas for inexpensive "dates" for couples or friends, compiled by Dr. Barb Brock at Eastern Washington

University. They are short on cash but long on creating memories.

- Make up an invitation with candy bars. (For example, You'll *Snicker* with *Almond Delight* when you see the *Milky Way!*) Deliver the invitation and invite the friend for a walk to the park. Then, chow down! Suggestions: Heath Bar, Butterfingers, M & M's, O-Henry, Babe Ruth, Mr. Goodbar, and Mounds.

- A tape-recorded message on a cassette was left in an envelope in the prospective date's mailbox. The rather poetic and flowery message stated the recipient should be ready for all seasons, wearing comfortable shoes, and waiting at the door at 3:00 on Sunday afternoon. After a LONG walk, the date had prepared a treat—hot fudge sundaes with huckleberry jam and toasted nuts for toppings. Hot fudge for summer, ice cream for winter, huckleberry jam for spring, and toasted nuts for fall.

- One spouse sent an invitation cut in the shape of a bicycle. The couple met at a pre-determined location and cycled to a nearby park. A picnic of cheese sandwiches, oreo cookies, and juice boxes followed.

Several groups offer marriage workshops designed for couples with good marriages who want to renew the "spark" :
- Worldwide Marriage Encounter, 1-800-795-5683.
- International Lutheran Marriage Encounter, 1-800-235-1010.
- United Marriage Encounter, 1-800-334-8920.
- Baptist Marriage Encounter, 1-800-795-LOVE.

Friendship Enhancers

Still need more ideas on fun ways to get together with adults? How about these ideas?

Ideas for a Creative Life

- The invitation was for a friend to make fortune cookies. Each person wrote ten "fortunes" to be placed inside the cookies. They made and baked the cookies with "fortunes" tucked inside. Then, they dressed up in "mysterious-looking" clothing and walked around the neighborhood delivering the cookies to other friends or neighbors.

- A prospective date received invitations in three library books. The rules said to return the books to the library and go to the location of their call numbers. At the library, a little gift had been tucked in between the books. After the gift was located, the couple checked out a scary book, a funny one, and a Christian book and brought them home to read excerpts aloud.

- "Meet me in the pool for a dugout canoe adventure, dressed in loin skins OR swimming attire," read the invitation written on a piece of birch bark. A free kayak class was being offered at the local university, and this couple signed up.

- A small kite woven from paper was taped to the bathroom mirror inviting "the man of the house" for the cheapest, most thrilling, high-flying time imaginable. With dime-store kites and a bag of chips, the couple spent the afternoon playing until one kite broke its string and the other slipped out of its owner's hand! They spent the next thirty minutes trying to chase down the kites. At last, they collapsed in laughter from the whole experience.

- A golf ball sufficed as an invitation and was "tossed" through an open window to the prospective date. It read, "Meet me at the local miniature golf center for a rip-roaring game of golf." Following the event, homemade macaroons made to look like golf balls were served "with tee."

> Want a practical, worthwhile activity to do with your spouse? Why not get together to donate blood?

Preserving Memories

How often have you regaled your children with stories of "When I was your age..."? After a while they simply roll their eyes and humor you by pretending interest. (I still think my stories about my boyfriend's pet monkey sitting on my head while we drove to school are funny, but not everyone in the family agrees!)

Family memories are important, but after awhile become distorted. You can keep the memories bright by creating a family time capsule. Simply have each family member collect three to four significant items to place in your "capsule."

One family gave everyone an empty three-pound coffee can with a plastic snap-on lid. After placing the items inside, they used duct tape to seal the lids. Each can was put in a plastic bag, and all the cans were stored in a heavy-duty plastic storage container.

Encourage family members to choose meaningful items for the time capsule, perhaps with a written explanation of the item's importance. Recently *Baby Talk Magazine* asked readers to tell what they'd put in a time capsule to be opened in sixty years. The top ten items included:

Photographs	Disposable diapers
Diaper Genie	*Baby Talk Magazine*
Medical bills	Barney paraphernalia
What to Expect books	Current day's newspaper
List of current baby expenses	Tylenol

After putting selected items in the storage container, bury it in a safe spot or store in your attic with the warning: "Do not open until (date)!" Be sure to give several people specific directions as to the time capsule's location.

Open the capsule every ten years to rekindle memories. Feel free to add or change items, since this activity is an ongoing process.

Be sure to include an up-to-date photo as you seal your time capsule!

Go Green

As the world population grows, it becomes increasingly important to preserve the environment. Since we're stewards of God's world, our actions set the stage for future generations and their attitudes toward recycling and conservation. In some cases, children come home from school adamant about recycling newspapers and plastics, while other times adults are the ones who decide to recycle. "Go Green" in your home with some of these ideas:

• Purchase cloth grocery bags and let children decorate them. Use these instead of paper or plastic bags. Personalized canvas bags make practical Christmas gifts.

- If going for a family walk, take along a bag to collect litter on the path.

- Save empty shampoo bottles to use as squirt guns in the summer.

- Plant a tree or shrub in honor of a birthday, graduation, or birth of a child. This is a lasting tribute to mark a special event.

- Have children design bookmarks with a recycling theme. Include these in your Christmas cards as a reminder to family and friends about the importance of our environment. One family printed a list of holiday recycling tips and included it as a gift tag on presents they gave.

- Collect tiny tree saplings from the woods and nurture them in your house. When they become sturdy, transplant them to your yard or ask permission to plant them in a local park.

- Set aside a family nature preserve, even if it's only a wooden tub on your deck. Fill with rocks, dirt, and flowers to attract a variety of small animals. Add a few bird feeders and a birdbath or something from which birds can drink. You might be lucky enough to see nature up close in the form of worms, butterflies, and ladybugs.

Children can join a club called "Kids for Saving Earth," Box 47247, Plymouth, MN 55447-0247, Phone: (612) 525-0002.

Obtain a free list of fifty handbooks of science and math activities from: GEMS, Lawrence Hall of Science, University of California, Berkeley, CA 94720.

Pizza Picnics

The sun shone brightly as crocus peeked up through the dirt. A group of preschoolers waited for their parents to pick them up after a fun-filled morning at school. One eager four year old hugged her mother and asked, "Mom—it finally stopped raining—can we go on a picnic today?" Her mother's response? "Don't be silly. It's May. You can only go on picnics in the summer. Where do you get such foolish ideas?"

Picnics provide a break from routines. You may only travel to your backyard, but the experience of eating outdoors transforms an ordinary meal into a special occasion. One of our family's favorite picnics involved packing a gingham tablecloth and juice and picking up a pizza before heading to the park. Though it was unplanned, to our surprise two other families soon arrived carrying their take-out pizzas, also!

- For variety, check out the day camping site at a local campground. These facilities offer clean restrooms and playgrounds.

- Take along a nature arts and crafts book for some impromptu activities. Bring a magnifying glass to observe bugs.

- Use small cotton dishtowels as napkins. They wash easily and mop up spills better than paper towels.

- Keep a spare blanket and a picnic basket in the car. If you have silverware, plates, and cups readily available, it's possible to have spontaneous picnics. Just stop in a deli to get sandwich makings and then head for the park.

- Don't worry about the chores that await you at home. They'll still be there after the picnic.

No picnic would be complete without reading *The Teddy Bear's Picnic* by Jimmy Kennedy and Alexandra Day, Green Tiger Press.

Two for Tea?

A mother facing communication problems with her thirteen-year-old daughter tried various ways to encourage her to talk. Nothing seemed to work until one day, after school, she set the table with a lace tablecloth and added a bouquet of fresh flowers. She greeted her daughter with, "Hi, Melissa, I have some tea and banana bread in the kitchen, if you'd like to join me." Melissa glanced at the table, gave a quick, "No thanks," and headed upstairs to the phone. Undaunted, her mother arranged the tea table three days in a row. Finally, Melissa sat down and joined her. Six months later, this ritual takes place two to three times a week. Now they are talking during these uninterrupted mother-daughter conversations.

The British are masters at slowing down the pace of a busy day by setting aside a few minutes for afternoon tea. Perhaps tea time would work in your family. It represents a chance to create a cozy atmosphere of food and communication.

If you don't like tea, don't worry.

- Tea isn't the only drink served. Hot chocolate, warm milk, or even a clear soup serve the same purpose.
- Presentation is important. Light a candle, purchase a few inexpensive yet "fancy" cups, and play soothing background music.

- Invite a few friends for afternoon tea. Even young boys can enjoy a short, formal time before they race off to ride bikes. Serve football-shaped cookies and watch them come to attention. A few pieces of crustless toast and a bowl of fresh fruit complete the tea.

- For younger children this subdued atmosphere is the ideal time to read a short Bible story. A Bible verse at each place setting is a nice touch. Jesus often took time to get away from his fast-paced life. A tea party is the catalyst to slow down and experience a few minutes of calm with our children.

> *The Five Love Languages of Children* by Gary Chapman and Ross Campbell, Northfield Publishing, helps people develop better relationships with children.

Continuing Traditions

"**B**ut Dad, we always go to Lake Carumba on Labor Day. We can't change!" How often have you heard children plead to continue the same traditions, year after year? The sense of family rituals and traditions creates a feeling of security in children. There's a warm fuzzy feeling knowing Grandpa takes the kids to the county fair every year and buys them all the cotton candy they want.

Your family may have special traditions for holidays and birthdays. Perhaps your tradition is for the birthday person to wake up in a room full of balloons. Some families open just one present on Christmas Eve. Everyone gets the same gift, and everyone knows each box contains a new pair of pajamas.

Daily life can become very mundane unless we create opportunities for family traditions. Consider some of these ways to strengthen family traditions and ties:

- Pick one day of the year as a family slumber party. Gather up sleeping bags (foam pads for adults to avoid aching backs!), and spread out on the living room floor for a night of fun.
- Designate a day as "Annual Family Day." Think of ways to celebrate the joy of simply being a family. Choose a specific meal or restaurant and participate in a family activity.
- Even everyday rituals are significant. One mother always wakes her children with a small, tinkling bell. At dinner, another family shares the best thing that happened that day.

Traditions create a sense of security and permanence for children. It's easier to understand God's steadfast and continuous love when children know certain special events will happen on a regular basis.

Sit down with your family and make a list of your family traditions. Which traditions should you celebrate more often?

All the World's a Stage

A high school teacher in an average, middle-class district asked students how many had attended a live theater performance. To her surprise, only six out of a class of twenty-four had ever gone to a ballet, play, or symphony. Yet twenty students eagerly shared their rock concert experiences.

Live theater gives children exposure to a world beyond cartoons and television sitcoms. The anticipation as the curtain parts, the overture begins, and live people appear on stage fuels imagination and creativity. Plays suitable for children evoke questions about costumes and set designs. Just how did they get that big pirate ship on stage in *Pirates of Penzance*? Did people really wear huge, billowing dresses like Anna's in *The King and I*?

While most children seldom perform on stage, they will gain an appreciation for people who do by attending live theater. By the time Sondra was three, we purchased season tickets for a musical comedy series of six plays. Since that time, her love of theater includes watching performances at local elementary schools to Broadway productions. As with any new experience, preparing your children for what they are about to see will enhance the experience.

- Explain to children ahead of time what to expect. A professional theater production of *The Wizard of Oz* requires different behavior than a sibling's backyard production.
- Read about the play or get a recording if it's a musical. Familiarity with the story line helps the children follow the story and thus maintain attention.
- Make play-going a special occasion by dressing up. When Sondra was younger, she'd dress as her favorite character from the play. Put on your Sunday best clothes to help create a feeling of "This is a special occasion."
- Instruct children not to talk during the performance. Often youngsters feel as if they're home watching a video, and they speak out whenever they feel like it.

- Once you're at the play, if it is inappropriate or too long for children's attention spans, leave at intermission.

Music Magic

Music soothes the savage beast and it also provides the opportunity to communicate, laugh, and share. Music appreciation goes beyond the structured lessons we experienced as children. Children have the natural ability to make up their own songs or beat on a box with their own distinct sense of rhythm. In a creative environment, children freely express themselves through a variety of musical possibilities. If you don't have instruments, snap your fingers, click your tongue, or slap your knees. Let yourself get silly.

Even if you are tone deaf and never had a music lesson in your life, there are ways to foster creativity and self-expression in your child through music.

- Play a variety of music in your home. Borrow music or go to the library for tapes and CDs of jazz, polka, disco, Broadway musicals, and Chinese folk music. If you've never listened to Black Gospel music, try it. You're in for a treat!
- Don't worry if you can't sing on key. Children love your participation more than perfect tonal quality.
- If a child makes up a song, offer to write down the words so it can be sung again and again.
- Record your child singing or tapping out the beat to a song. (If you are really brave—record yourself singing a song.)
- Put on a variety of music and conduct a family limbo contest. Get ready for some sore muscles!

- See if you can obtain a hymnal from your church, or better yet, purchase one for your home. Call the church office on Friday and ask which hymns are scheduled for the Sunday service. Practice ahead of time with your children so they can sing and feel more a part of the service.

> *Finger Plays and Action Chants* by Pearce-Evetts Productions has new and traditional songs and fingerplays. Cassette and illustrated book are included.

Low-Cost Instruments

I'll never forget the time Allan and Sondra met me at the airport dressed as a "two-person band." They wore cymbals attached to their knees, bells on their wrists, and were holding maracas while playing harmonicas. Their musical ability didn't win any awards, but they did get attention for their originality.

If you don't have traditional instruments, look around the house for supplies to create your own.

- Rhythm sticks are simply two dowels or pieces of PVC pipe. You can cut an old broom handle into twelve-inch lengths if you don't want to purchase new wood.

- Using a heavy-duty staple gun, or carpenter's glue, cover two pieces of easy-to-hold wood with sandpaper. Children enjoy "swooching" the two pieces of wood back and forth.

- Empty film canisters filled with unpopped popcorn or rice make great shakers. Be sure to tape the top shut if young children might accidentally swallow the contents.

- Use empty coffee cans or round oatmeal containers for drums.
- Put a few rocks in an empty tin can. Cover the top with duct tape for an extra loud shaker. Great for outdoor use.

Look for ways to incorporate music into everyday routines. Instead of saying grace before meals, sing a favorite hymn. One family passes the time in the car by creating their own verses to "If You're Happy and You Know It." Squabbling dissipates when people sing "If you're cranky and you know it, stick out your tongue." (They also get strange looks from people driving by their car.)

Classical Recordings:

- *Pictures at an Exhibition,* by Modest Maussorgsky
- *The Classical Child,* Metro Music
- *The Nutcracker Suite,* Peter Tchaikovsky

Quick Creative Concepts

Children love imagining and pretending. Dressing up like Dorothy in *The Wizard of Oz* or joining Indiana Jones on a wild adventure stirs a child's imagination. On those days when your children are restless and can't think of anything to do, a little structure may be needed. Often, suggesting a few ideas and spending ten to fifteen minutes participating in those activities gives children the focus needed to entertain themselves. Here are a few low-key suggestions to get children thinking in a creative way.

- Invent a nonsense machine using five or six children as machine parts. The first child stands and lifts one leg up and down. The next child "connects" to the machine by raising his arm back and forth in rhythm to the first child. The machine gets more complex as other children use their bodies to make a moving, whimsical contraption. Sound effects are even more fun.

- What would it be like if you and your best friend were the last people on earth?

- If you were designing the next spaceship for a *Star Wars* film, what would it look like?

- What do you think you'll look like in twenty-five years? Draw a picture of yourself as you think you might look.

- What are twenty uses for a piece of Scotch tape?

- How can you play volleyball using three balls and eight children?

- Create a new candy. Describe the taste. How will you wrap it?

- Draw your world as seen through the eyes of a snake.

- Make a list of things that are flat.

- Create a coat of arms about your life.

- Make up a rap song about your best friend.

- What would be your ideal meal and where would you eat it?

- If you had a chance to spend all day with a famous person, who would it be?

> Brainstorm with your children about activities they can do with little preparation or supplies. Keep the list in a prominent place for easy reference when you want ten to fifteen minutes of fun.

Bubbles Galore

Who hasn't enjoyed blowing bubbles through the little plastic blower inside the jar of bubble solution? Take the commercial solution one step further by creating a variety of bubble shapes and sizes using various tools. Once your bubbles are in the air, don't just watch them float—get moving!

- Blow bubbles on a plate and gently place in the freezer to create frozen bubbles.
- Give everyone one of those New Year's Eve party blowers. Blow many bubbles and have fun trying to pop them with your party blower. As it unfurls, you should be able to pop numerous bubbles at once.
- Set up a simple obstacle course in the house. Using a paper plate or piece of cardboard, gently fan a bubble around the coffee table, next to the couch, through the kitchen, and so forth. See who can get a bubble the farthest through the obstacle course before it pops.
- Blow bubbles outside when it's dark. Shine a flashlight on them and see their swirling color patterns.
- Spread a small amount of bubble solution on the kitchen counter. This gives a bondable surface to work on. Blow bubbles directly on top of the counter. Each bubble will attach to the counter as well as the bubbles next to it, creating unique geometrical shapes.
- On a hot day, give everyone a squirt gun. Blow bubbles and pop them with water from the squirt gun.
- Use a variety of items to dip in the bubble solution. Flyswatters, plastic strawberry baskets, and even hula hoops help create bubbles.

Bubble Recipe

1 cup water

2 T liquid detergent

1 T glycerin (available in drug stores)

1/2 tsp. sugar

Mix well and let sit for 24 hours for best bubbles.

Splish-Splash

B ath time in our house means my husband and I get close to forty-five minutes of uninterrupted conversation when Sondra is in the tub.

To make bath time enjoyable, try adding some variety. Rotate the usual bathtub toys. By removing half of them for a few weeks, they'll seem fresh and new when they reappear. Purchase some soap crayons. Most discount stores carry these colored bars of soap for "drawing" on the sides of the tub. Simply splash water on the finished painting to clean up. This is one time painting without paper is encouraged! Here are some additional ideas:

- Provide a variety of unusual items and let your child guess if they sink or float.
- Set out a few plastic glasses filled with various shades of colored water. Children enjoy mixing the colors to create their own secret blends.
- Collect a variety of different sizes and shapes of sponges. There's something fascinating about squeezing a wet object and suddenly seeing it is dry.

- To calm an active child, dim the lights and set up a few candles (with constant adult supervision) to create a dim, soothing atmosphere.
- One mother placed a board across the tub to serve as a table. Her daughter enjoyed a bedtime snack while relaxing in the tub.
- Provide snorkels and a mask for bathtub exploration.
- Let older children use plastic straws to blow bubbles.
- Throw some doll clothes into the tub for an old-fashioned hand-washing session.
- Drop a few ice cubes into the tub and observe how quickly they melt.
- Set up a nonbreakable mirror and encourage your child to create shampoo hair creations.

When running bath water, always finish with cold water. That way, if your child leans against the faucet, the drops of water that might come out will be cold rather than hot.

Take II

Sometimes, as I watch my independent seven year old ride a bike, rollerblade, or read a book, I find it hard to remember her as a helpless baby. That's when the videotapes come out for a night of "Oh! Look how we gave her a bath in the sink," and "She looks so cute in her baby Easter Bunny costume." I'm enthralled with the main subject of our home videos, but dismayed at the overall amateur quality. They certainly are videos only close family members enjoy! We won't give Steven Spielberg any competition; however, here's how to improve the quality of your home videos:

- Read the manual that comes with your video camera. Yes, that sounds boring, but it contains valuable information on lighting, zoom, and special effects.

- Hold the camera as steady as possible. Rather than jerking the camera back and forth to follow your child kicking a soccer ball, use a tripod. Slowly pan the camera to catch the action.

- Look for unusual angles. Three minutes of your son playing chopsticks on the piano is cruel and unusual punishment. Break up the scene by filming the entire piano or a close-up of his hands. Reflect his intense concentration by shooting his face while you lie on the floor for an upward angle.

- Professional filmmakers change scenes or angles every five to ten seconds. This adds interest for viewers. Try a zoom shot. Film an interesting aspect of the background.

- Remember to record everyday events. It's natural to film dance recitals and baby dedications, but in the years to come, you'll enjoy watching children brush their teeth and walk the dog. Many parents even videotape close-ups of cherished art projects.

Sometimes it seems too much trouble to keep batteries recharged and the video handy. Years from now, your children will howl with laughter as they see themselves in diapers and learning to eat with a spoon. Hopefully they'll also sense the love and care you put into their childhood.

What To Do With All Those Pictures

Professional photographers suggest tossing two-thirds of your photos. They know it's difficult to get good photos of children that even strangers will want to admire. When Sondra needs a new head-shot for her commercial work, the photographer shoots thirty-six pictures to get one we use. Since most of us can't bear to toss any photographs, here are a few ways to get them out of those shoeboxes.

- Find pictures with clear faces of family and friends. Close-ups work best. Cut carefully around the face and glue to the top of a popsicle stick. Cut out clothes from fabric and paper to create real-life puppets.

- Collect all the squinty-eyed, funny-face pictures to use as homemade greeting cards. Add humorous captions for cards that rival Hallmark.

- Print out twelve calendar pages for the upcoming year, leaving a space for photos. Mail calendar pages to eleven other relatives, asking them to decorate their own page with photos. Collect, make copies for everyone, and assemble into a one-of-a-kind family photographic calendar.

- Purchase plain-colored, plastic placemats. Give one to each family member along with a stack of photographs. Each person selects pictures, cuts them in unusual angles or shapes, and glues them to their placemat. Cover with clear adhesive contact paper for personalized funny face placemats.

- Select a favorite picture and glue to white foam core (available at any art store). Carefully cut around photo to create a 3-D picture.

- If your family enjoys card games, make a customized deck. Purchase a set of cards with a plain back side. Cut out fifty-two pictures and glue onto the cards.

- Rather than displaying all your photos in one giant album, create albums on particular subjects. We have photo albums designated for birthdays, sports, and live performances. My favorite is a photo album strictly for pictures of Sondra and me in matching outfits.

- Purchase an inexpensive cardboard mat frame. Take photographs and cut around faces and bodies. Glue these cutouts all around the frame, overlapping, to create a photo frame collage.

Want the entire world to see a picture of your family? Join ParentSoup for free on the Internet and they'll display your favorite "refrigerator photo." www.parentsoup.com.

Block Versatility

"What are you able to build with your blocks? Castles and palaces, temples and docks. Rain may keep raining and others go roam, let the sofa be mountains and the carpet be sea, there I'll establish a city for me."

Robert Louis Stevenson

The versatility of blocks is endless:

- Have children sit back-to-back with a sibling or yourself. Work for three to four minutes creating a structure out of blocks. At the designated time, switch places and add on to your partner's structure. After a few minutes, stop and see how your original structure changed when someone else worked on it.

- Ask your child to use the blocks to create an ideal room for themselves. Incorporate doll house furniture and other props. Build bunk beds, swimming pools, and so forth.

- If you have a guinea pig or hamster, have your child build a maze and let your pet explore for food. Maintain close supervision so the pet doesn't get confused or stressed.

- Supply a few boards to use as ramps. Block play takes on a new dimension when cars and toys roll down ramps.

- Walk through the neighborhood. When you return home, ask your child to use blocks to make a map on the floor. Use masking tape for roads and incorporate your house, the neighbor's house, and other landmarks.

- Children can use the blocks to create two identical mazes, side by side. Have a race to see who can blow air through a straw to move a Ping-Pong ball from one end of the maze to the other.

- Wrap a few blocks in aluminum foil. Build a structure and turn off the lights. Use a flashlight to see the shiny reflection of your child's block creation.

Puzzlemania

Hopefully by now you see that the process of family togetherness is more important than the end result of the project. So your craft project didn't turn out as perfect as the magazine photo, but you had a good laugh when the cat rolled on top of Dad's play dough creation. The experience of being together as a family, enjoying a simple activity, is the foundation for raising creative, adventurous children.

A mother of three active boys stated, "One day when my kids were squabbling, I realized I was guilty of always telling them to go play on their own. As a parent, it's my responsibility to take time to play with them, also." This parent didn't feel comfortable with rough and tumble play, so she simply included her sons in an activity she enjoyed—puzzles. They went on a shopping excursion to thrift shops and garage sales to purchase puzzles in a wide range of difficulty. Soon even the five year old joined in, talking and sharing as they all put together puzzles.

Try these ideas to add interest when working on puzzles:

- Organize a puzzle exchange with friends. Almost every family closet contains seldom-used puzzles.
- If you have very young children, set them up next to you to work their own large-piece puzzles so they feel a part of the family.
- Let children make their own puzzles. Glue magazine pictures or photographs on a piece of lightweight cardboard. Let dry and cut into a random assortment of shapes.
- Many photo stores offer to make puzzles out of your favorite photo. They enlarge the picture, mount it, and cut it into pieces like a regular puzzle.

A Place to Dream

Need a few suggestions to get young builders off to a strong start in creating their own secret hideaway?

- If you live in a dry climate, a large appliance box remains durable for weeks. Lay it on its side and cut a flap for the door. Here's the fun part: Use branches and leaves to camouflage the box so it truly is a secret place. (Of course, if you have a beautifully manicured lawn, it will be a bit obvious to suddenly see a leaf-covered box in the middle. But why not create a conversation piece for the neighborhood?)

- Lean-tos provide a quick and easy way to create a fort. Use an old screen door or scrap wood to lean against the side of a permanent building. Try leaning several strong branches and "weaving" smaller twigs in and out.

- Several appliance boxes taped together make a spaceship fort. Glue on cans or small boxes for a control center. Tape the boxes with duct tape, which adds to the silver spaceship decor.

- On a snowy day, roll large snowballs and stack them on top of each other in a "U" shape. Add a large board over the structure, and you have a modern-day igloo fort.

Offer gentle support to your child as he or she builds the fort. Experimenting is a natural part of the construction process; however, you don't want your child totally frustrated. My daughter wanted to build a fort with a thatched roof. After several futile attempts with leftover straw from the sheep pen, I stepped in to suggest an alternative roof plan, which satisfied her.

Donate some old carpets or cushions to add to the fort's interior. Don't forget to bring a "housewarming" gift of cookies and juice to dedicate the completion of their project.

The Kid's Guide to Building Forts
by Tom Birdseye, Harbinger House.

Hit the Books

The media constantly stresses the importance of reading to our children. So we dutifully sit down with a squirming toddler and look at picture books, asking, "What does the cow say?" Yet, as our children get older, we're so caught up in everyday routines, we forget to read for sheer pleasure.

A mother with two preteens makes a point of getting up a few minutes early to have her own time for reading and a cup of coffee. Then, while her children eat breakfast, she reads to them. It can be anything from a newspaper article on a woman with ten-inch fingernails to an excerpt from her Bible study workbook.

My daughter loves looking at the series of large picture books, put out by Life Publishing, called "A Day in the Life of _____." The books show hundreds of photographs depicting a day in the life of China, Ireland, the United States, and even Hollywood. We both enjoy the colorful pictures and short explanations, so the reading process is done for pleasure, not out of duty. *National Geographic* magazine follows the same format of colorful photos with short descriptions.

One principal told a group of parents, "*You* have a homework assignment every night. Spend at least twenty minutes reading *enthusiastically* to your children."

- Keep books with short stories available in the car. Take them along while waiting with children at the dentist or barber shop.
- Show children how information is gained by reading the back of packages or the fine print on a sale coupon.
- Read your child's baby book to him or her.

The Internet and computers open a world of information, but nothing compares to sitting side by side, holding a book together and discovering the wonders of the printed page.

Read Aloud Bible Stories by Ella Lindvall, Moody Press.
The Read-Aloud Handbook by Jim Trelease, Penguin Books.
The New Read-Aloud Handbook by Jim Trelease, Penguin Books.

Reading With Enthusiasm

OK, as parents we should read enthusiastically to our children. But how do we maintain enthusiasm after the twentieth (or 200th) reading of *Green Eggs and Ham*?

A mother of a seven year old confessed, "I used to get bored reading the same books over and over. Finally I decided to pretend I was a famous actress making a Books on Tape series. Now I read with dramatic pauses, vocal inflection, and enthusiasm. Jordan loves it and so do I."

Demonstrate to your children the excitement of reading by making books come alive. Try some of these ideas:

- Replace the main character with your child's name throughout the story.
- Watch the newspaper for announcements about upcoming visits from children's authors. A chance to meet a favorite author makes reading take on special significance.
- Read a new book and stop in the middle. Ask your child to guess the outcome.
- If the book mentions cornbread muffins, find a recipe and make a batch for dinner.

- Reading about horses? Arrange for a family horseback riding trip.
- Let your children know about the books *you* read. Share a funny incident in your book, or read a short paragraph. Your example shows children reading is for everyone.
- Ask your child to write a book. Read the story often, no matter how basic.
- Select books of interest to you as well as your child. The library's selection of oversized books provide information for adults, with large pictures to hold a child's attention. You'll find pictorial books on subjects ranging from mountain climbing to unusual animals to jewelry designs. Learning the eating habits of the aardvark provides relief from another repetition of *Green Eggs and Ham!*

To emphasize the importance of books, one family always purchased one hardcover, coffee table book for their children's birthdays. The expense and thought to subject matter showed the value the family placed on books.

More With Less

Jesus promises us an abundant life, not a life filled with an abundance of things. After living overseas, it shocked me to return to the States and see how many "things" children have.

Are fifteen stuffed animals really necessary?

A recent magazine article described a father who told his children they could have ten toys. (A set of LEGOs or blocks counted as one toy.) Anytime a new toy was purchased or received as a gift, one toy had to be donated to charity. Books and art supplies were always available, but the children had to make hard choices about their dolls, cars, and other toys. He found this resulted in his children using their creativity when playing and also resulted in fewer toys to pick up!

When our daughter was two and a half, we asked relatives to chip in and buy her a set of wooden blocks for Christmas. Now, four years later, the blocks still serve as the foundation for horse stables, doll houses, and dance floors.

Anytime children improvise or adapt, creative thinking skills develop. Turning an ordinary shoe box into an undersea treasure chest requires thought about where to get supplies and how to use them.

Rather than racing to the store to purchase the toy of the week, consider using that driving time to play a game or shoot baskets with your ten year old.

The following items provide opportunities for open ended play:
- Assorted boxes
- Colored paper (fluorescent colors are great)
- Pipe cleaners
- Toobers and Zots (interconnecting foam shapes)
- Non-motorized cars and trucks
- Dress-up clothes

Practice "voluntary simplicity" and see if stress decreases and family time increases.

Folkman's Puppets Catalog offers unique, realistic puppets. Haven't you always wanted a sloth, stingray, or platypus puppet? The best part is: no batteries needed! Call 1-800-773-1115.

New Experiences, New Adventures

You take your son to his first orchestra concert. Your daughter accompanies her dad to work for the day. You are asked to organize a school fundraiser. New experiences provoke excitement along with classic first-day-of-school anxiety. Anytime you expose children to a new experience, prepare them in advance. "I took my six year old to an expensive production of the *Nutcracker,* and she fidgeted the whole time," complained one mother. To avoid this problem and prepare the child for a new experience:

- Ask your child: What do you think it will be like to see a play? Your child's answer gives you the chance to remove any false perceptions he or she might have. When I took my five year old to a Broadway production of *Beauty and the Beast,* she was disappointed to learn she could not go up on stage and join the cast. To ease her disappointment, we arranged for her to go on the set after the play. We took her picture on stage.

- Let children see you experience new situations also. Tell them about your discomfort at learning a new computer program or dealing with a new supervisor. New experiences make us vulnerable, and this is a chance to demonstrate creative thinking.

- If the new experience involves a crowded setting, designate a specific location to meet in case you become separated.
- Read books to your child on the subject. A parent told me, "My five year old practiced a dance for three months in her dance class for a recital. She talked and talked about this recital. It was only after I read to her the book *Harriet's Recital* by Nancy Carlson that I realized she had no idea what a recital was!"
- If attending a concert or play, call ahead to check on the possibility of a behind-the-scenes tour.

A little preparation ahead of time increases the chance of a positive experience when attempting something new. Your child gains confidence, whether auditioning for the school chorus or eating lunch with a new student.

> "When someone does something well, applaud!
> You will make two people happy."
>
> Samuel Goldwyn

Choices, Choices, Choices

"Youth can be destructive or constructive, and they're going to be one or the other so you might as well provide the means for them to be creative," states Seattle author Michael Meade. Several years ago I spent an afternoon with four children, ranging in age from six to eleven. All four had spent most of their young lives in and out of foster homes. As I brought out a variety of craft materials, they complained: "This is stupid! I'm not making anything out of that junk. You probably want me to read the directions, don't you?" When they saw it was up to them to decide how to paint the Frisbees and decorate painters' hats, their tone changed. Slowly they asked if it was "OK" to mix white and black paint to make gray. While they wanted specific directions, I kept telling them to use the supplies in the way they wished. The six year old had never used glue before and was fascinated by the way the cap worked to release the glue. It was one of the few times these children had been given choices. All their lives, adults had told them what to do and even where they would live. Now they were allowed to make choices with no fear of punishment. Their looks of proud accomplishment as they displayed their masterpieces were worth the mess in the room.

While these four children were in an unusual situation, your children benefit from making choices also. Here's how to let them do it:

- Let toddlers decide between milk or juice.
- Let early school-aged kids decide if they want a bedtime story or an audio tape.
- Let middle schoolers decide on a week's dinner menus.
- Set out school clothes the night before for young children. Let them decide what to wear, after giving them a few basic guidelines.
- Give them the choice of vacuuming the car or raking leaves.
- After church, let them decide if they want to go to the park or ride bikes. Let them choose between a shower or bath.
- Do they want to sign up for soccer or swim team?
- Ask their opinion about selecting birthday presents for friends.

When children feel they can occasionally make choices on their own, they are more accepting of the times when you have firm rules.

Why Can't We Live in Paris?

We are all familiar with Paul's words in Philippians 4:11 about being content in whatever situation God places us. Yet, no matter how hard we try, there stirs a longing in us to move to the country, to move to the city, to move to a different city or even travel the world before retirement. Then reality sets in and we get back to living in our same community and learning to be content.

That's not such a bad option. Help your children (and yourself) gain a new appreciation for where you live by creating a hometown documentary video.

Relatives living long distances away or overseas missionaries might delight in seeing everyday scenes of your world. Get your family together and form the "Clark Family Production Company." List the everyday places you go, and assign a camera crew (family members) to film and document the scenes. If your four year old chooses the playground for her segment, film scenes of her climbing the monkey bars and swinging by herself. Then let her film the rest of the park while you add commentary.

Point out to your family how the things we take for granted are a novelty for some people. One family sent a tape to relatives living in rural Holland that included an evening stop at the 7-11 for a Slurpee. The relatives watched the tape in amazement, because stores staying open past 6:00 P.M. are unheard of in Holland. If you're lucky, you'll get a similar tape in return, so you can see how people live in other cultures and environments.

To keep the video interesting:

- Keep dialogue to a minimum. It's easier to watch the tape without hearing giggling, and "I don't know what to say," in the background.

- Include typical places such as the library, the computer lab at school, and the post office.

- Don't forget to shoot footage of your bathroom, if the tape is going to someone living in an undeveloped country!

Stay at Home Drive-Ins

Set up your own neighborhood drive-in theater in your yard. An outdoor theater provides welcome relief from the heat on hot summer nights. Invite neighbors to attend and bring their blankets and lawn chairs to sit on. Part of the fun is setting up with your family all the necessary paraphernalia like flashlights, portable cribs for babies, and snacks for the event. If your garage door or house is white, you have an instant screen on which to project movies.

The one difficulty may be locating a 16 mm projector and reel-to-reel movies. Before the days of video, these were easy to find. Your public library or school is still a good resource. Set up the projector, wait until dark, and let the fun begin.

Another option is to haul a TV outdoors and show videos. Some groups enjoy a potluck before the movie, while others only want snacks. One enterprising ten year old rode his bike from neighbor to neighbor, announcing the movie night and letting people know a popcorn and lemonade stand would be available. He did a booming business as people smelled and purchased the freshly popped popcorn.

For additional atmosphere, create a theme around the movie.

- If viewing *Mary Poppins,* get one mother to dress up as the famous nanny with a black coat and umbrella and greet guests.
- Serve Reese's Pieces if showing the movie *E. T.*
- Before showing *The Sound of Music,* have everyone stand and sing a rousing chorus of "Do-Re-Me."
- Of course, you need to pass around a variety of chocolate candy if watching *Willy Wonka and the Chocolate Factory.*

> If a film projector is unavailable, ask families to bring twenty family slides. Show the slides on the side of the house and enjoy a mini slide show of family activities.

Making Bill Cosby Proud

Bill Cosby does an amusing public service radio commercial telling how he almost burned down his house with a new chemistry set. First he establishes the importance of science exploration, then he begs his father to give back his chemistry set. Here are some science activities that are fun and are very low risk for your home.

- Sprinkle a few cotton balls with a variety of smells, such as a few drops of vinegar, cinnamon, shoe polish, or onion. Take turns closing your eyes and trying to identify the smells.

- A variation on this activity is to close your eyes, plug your nose, and taste samples of food. It's difficult to distinguish a peeled potato from a peeled apple when only using the taste buds.

- Collect a variety of magnets in different shapes and sizes. Lay out numerous objects on the table and have children guess which ones can be picked up with a magnet. Make your own mini magnet by straightening a paper clip. Rub a strong magnet over the paper clip in the same direction at least twenty-five to thirty times. You've now created a magnet that can pick up other lightweight items.

- Divide the family into two or three groups so younger children pair up with adults. Give each group one raw egg and one hour to design a container that will keep the egg intact when dropped from a second story window! You'll be amazed at the contraptions family members devise. Neighbors will wonder about all the cheering coming from your house as the eggs are dropped out of a window.

> *Silly Science, Strange and Startling Projects to Amaze Your Family and Friends* by Shar Levine and Leslie Johnstone, Wiley Press.
> *Kids's Squish Book,* Marlor Press, Inc.

Watch Out, Bill Nye

Many of us remember sitting in school, watching a film of Mr. Wizard perform science experiments. There he stood, with a no-nonsense attitude, wearing his suit, speaking in a monotone, explaining how gravity works. We were fascinated, nonetheless.

Today Bill Nye appears on television showing the wonders of science. Instead of wearing a suit, he dons scuba equipment and picks up underwater trash. Other times he belly-flops and swims through a giant mud puddle to demonstrate forward motion.

Bill Nye shows how science relates to our lives, even if it does get a bit messy. Foster scientific creativity in your children by performing some experiments of your own.

- Make some bathtime "fizz" by combining 3/4 cup baking soda, 1/2 cup cream of tartar, and 2 tablespoons cornstarch in a jar. Mix well. Add a few drops of perfume or peppermint extract. Keep the jar closed tightly. Next time you take a bath, add a few spoonfuls to the water for a tingly, refreshing experience.

- Cut a six-inch slit up the bottom half of a celery stalk. Stick one half in a jar of water dyed red. Place the other half in blue water. Wait overnight and see how the dyed water transforms the ordinary piece of celery into a colorful creation.

- For a truly unique science experiment, make up a batch of "Gak." This substance will amaze you with its strength, stretchiness, and pliability. This is a great birthday party activity also.

Gak the Great

Mix 1 cup cold water and 1 cup of Elmer's glue and stir. (Must use Elmer's). In a separate bowl, mix 1 tablespoon Boraxo with 1/2 cup very hot water (not boiling). You can add a few drops of food coloring to the water and Boraxo mixture. Add hot water mixture to the glue and water. Mix a few seconds, and suddenly the GAK forms! Keeps covered in the refrigerator for weeks.

Par Four

Early childhood educators know the importance of "Process, Not Results." A young child's experimentation with paints, brushes, and clay is important to his or her development. Working together with your children on a project produces endless opportunities for communication and creative problem solving.

Ask your children if they want to help construct a miniature golf course. Here's how:

- Look around the house and garage for everyday items that can be transformed into a perfect Par Four.
- Use a large piece of indoor-outdoor carpet for the putting green. One family simply pushed all their rec room furniture against the walls and set up their temporary golf course on the carpet. Instead of cutting holes in the carpet, they laid small boxes on their sides as cups.
- Ask a carpet store for the large cardboard tubes on which carpets are rolled. These make great dividers or "bumpers" to guide the

ball from one area to another. You can even design your course so the ball must pass through these tubes.

- Add interest by constructing a ramp that ends in the back of a toy truck. Mound some dirt or beach sand for the ball to travel across.
- Plastic PVC plumbing pipes come in an assortment of curved shapes. Elbows, Ys, and corners provide the twists and turns for balls to maneuver a variety of obstacles.

Arnold Palmer probably won't beg to play your course, but your children's memory of constructing a "major" miniature golf course will remain in their minds.

> "Children who are born into happy families grow up speaking love as their native language."
>
> Ashleigh Brilliant

Celebrating
Your
Children
With
Creativity

Celebrating Your Children

We've all heard our children moan, "It's not fair! There's Mother's Day and Father's Day—but never a Kids' Day!" Before you begin another mini-lecture about how every day is kids' day, let your children pick a day totally devoted to *them*. Some families give an entire day to each child, while others keep it simple by giving the designated child a favorite meal and activity.

In a casual way (so you don't put a damper on the excitement), set some guidelines. How much are you willing to spend? Do all activities need to take place at home? Can friends be invited for the celebration? A few guidelines when beginning this tradition prevent misunderstandings and hurt feelings.

One family with three children let each child pick a special day once a year. When it was "National Jason Day," he got to select his favorite meal, choose an at-home activity, go to bed one hour later, and receive a small gift. Each child knew the parameters for their special day. They, however, had a great amount of flexibility in choosing how to celebrate their day.

Other ideas for celebrating:

- Sneak into the child's room before he or she wakes up and decorate with balloons and streamers.
- Make a giant banner to hang over the kitchen table.
- Ask relatives to call and tell the child how special he or she is.

- Send a note to the child's classroom hinting about a surprise gift waiting at home after school.
- Bake a cake and let the special child use as much frosting as he or she wants to decorate it.

One mother of two sons who regularly celebrated National Kids' Day said the highlight of their special day was not having to brush their teeth at bedtime!

Children have a strong sense of security and well-being when you show them you care and they are special to you. An entire day of focused attention provides them positive memories for tough times.

Libraries Unlimited

Libraries used to be dark, quiet buildings dominated by stern-faced librarians. Today's libraries, however, are filled with numerous resources and activities that go far beyond stacks of books and magazines. Some libraries allow you to check out artwork, compact discs, videos, tapes, and even toys from a toy-lending center. To take maximum advantage of this free resource:

- Consider having a weekly family library night, including a stop for ice cream on the way home. Some families set a certain theme for their library nights. On "sports" night, every family member gets a book, magazine, or video relating to a sport. Some of their other categories include such topics as unusual animals, famous people, and musical instruments. Throughout the week discussions center around the chosen topic.
- Have a library scavenger hunt to discover its hidden resources.
- Attend a library's pajama story hour.

- Check out books on tape, computer programs, and CDs.
- Plan a small party celebrating a child's first library card.
- Take your children with you as you look for information on how to repair the car or build a new deck. They learn best by imitating parents.
- Give everyone only fifteen minutes to check out a funny book, record, or tape. Then spend the next day reading the books or listening to tapes.
- Plan an international night using library books as a source for recipes, traditions, and a mini geography lesson. One family held a German evening by making pretzels while listening to polkas. The evening concluded with a yodeling contest. It's a night they'll not soon forget.
- If your library doesn't have the book you want, ask them to order it from a larger branch. Even smaller libraries offer inter-library loans for hard-to-find books.

Money Making Library Cards: A national program called JumpStart encourages parents and teachers to help children get their first library cards. Children receiving a library card through JumpStart are eligible for $50,000 to a college expense fund. JumpStart, 50 High Ridge Ave., Ridgefield, CT 06877.

Fantasy Fun

"If you have built your castles in the air, your work need not be lost. Now put foundations under them." HENRY DAVID THOREAU

Your children probably have shelves full of building blocks, dolls, and the latest action figures. Yet they still come to you with sorrowful faces saying, "There's nothing to do!"

This is a perfect time to guide them in how to fill their time themselves. Rather than saying, "Find something to do," or, "I'll give you chores to do around the house," take a few minutes to brainstorm creative ideas for filling time.

- Get a clipboard or an official-looking notepad and ask your son to list some wild, expensive activities he could do. Of course, the list will include a trip to Disneyland and an extravagantly redecorated bedroom. Use the list as a springboard to learning. Ask, "How much does it cost to go to Disneyland?" Have your child check the Sunday travel section of the newspaper to compare rates. Encourage the child to use the Internet or send a postcard to the Anaheim Visitor and Convention Center for information on surrounding attractions. When the child has come up with costs, let him think of ways to raise enough money to pay for the dream vacation.
- If your daughter wants to redo her bedroom, begin by suggesting she cut out catalog pictures and design her own dream room. Then have her think of ways to adapt what's in the pictures into affordable ideas. Help her to see what's possible. Could she stencil a border around her door and windows? How about wallpapering one wall with a discounted roll of wallpaper? Would rearranging furniture create a new feeling in the room?
- Ask children to obtain information about an exotic location they'd like to visit.
- Have teens think about unique experiences they'd like to attempt: mountain climbing, traveling to Europe, sky diving. Obtain brochures to compare programs and costs.

- Read books about people who achieved great things. Find out how those individuals took a grandiose idea and worked until they were able to achieve their dreams.

Adapting Dreams

Take another look at your child's fantasy wish list and discuss with him or her how to adapt the ideas from fantasy to workable ideas. One aspiring ten-year-old actress wanted to see a Broadway musical. Since expense and distance made this impossible, her mother purchased tickets to a nearby college summer-stock production of *Fiddler on the Roof*. As an added bonus, the mother contacted the director, explained the situation, and was invited to bring her daughter to a rehearsal. She also got a personalized backstage tour. Her daughter's love for the theater was acknowledged with little cost but with plenty of individualized attention.

Use your child's wish list as a springboard to teach goal setting. List what each family member wants to accomplish within the next six months, two years, and six years. (Your toddler might be content to scribble on the folder that stores your lists.) This is a soul-searching time for adults, also. What do *you* want to be doing in six years? Have you always had a desire to go back to school, learn a foreign language, or refinish antique furniture? Share those dreams with your children, and then talk with them about how you have to accomplish them. Your goal setting will inspire your children to also set goals such as learning to ride a two-wheeler or getting up the courage to try out for cheerleading.

Other ideas about goal setting are:

- Read books about people who set goals and accomplished them.
- Share with your children the goals you had when you were younger. Did you reach your goals?
- Break down larger goals into smaller, manageable chunks. For example, if you've always wanted to write a book, begin by writing a short article for your denominational newsletter. Then expand to writing a magazine article. Soon you'll have skills and material to get your book on the best-seller list. (Well, we hope it will happen someday.) Show your children how to reach their larger goals by accomplishing many smaller goals. You never know, maybe your budding gymnast will be the next Mary Lou Retton.

Opening the Treasure Chest

Have you ever dreamed of finding a treasure chest filled with rare diamonds, pearls, and jewels? We have a treasure chest of opportunities to give to our children—a treasure chest of positive memories and experiences. When the world seems a hostile place, they can open that chest and take jewels of strength from the experiences you've shared as a family. Perhaps our income level may not be what we wish it were and the car may not be the latest model, but we can still be rich in life experiences. So here's a chance to start filling up your treasure chest:

- Set a small basket or box on the kitchen table. Keep paper and pencil close so each person can jot down something for which he or she is thankful. One evening read the notes before dinner.
- Be the catalyst to organize a family reunion. Rent a conference center or campground and invite family members to get together

for several days of fun. There are books describing ways to plan successful reunions. They often include helpful checklists and time lines to make planning easier.

- If you live in an area where trees change color in the fall, collect leaves and press them lightly with a warm iron. Pack them carefully and mail to friends living in arid climates.

- If your children attend residential day camp, mail a letter or care package to them at camp four or five days before they leave. (Then they'll get mail the first day of camp and will be the only one to get a letter.)

- Spend an evening together making a master list of family activities as simple as making homemade ice cream or drawing self portraits. Post the list on the refrigerator as a source of ideas when boredom hits.

- Set a goal to establish one new family tradition each year.

Fun and Games for Family Gatherings: With a Focus on Reunions by Adrienna Anderson, Reunion Research.

"The family was established long before the church. My duty is to my family first."
D.L. MOODY

The Reunion Planner by Linda Hoffman and Neal Barnett, Goodman Lauren Publishing.

Can Compassion Be Taught?

It's a sad commentary on our society that many schools mandate character and an ethics-related curriculum. Teachers must schedule time for lessons ranging from conflict resolution to morality. Schools find children have few skills for showing compassion to others. High schools increasingly require students to perform community service projects in order to graduate.

As Christians, we have Jesus' examples of caring and compassion to impart to our children. Opportunities exist on a regular basis for modeling empathy for others.

- Reinforce positive behavior. If children put part of their allowance in the offering plate or share a toy, praise them.
- When reading books, pause and ask your child, "How do you think the boy felt when kids made fun of him?" "What would you have said to him?"
- Let children observe you performing acts of kindness in spontaneous ways. Offer to carry groceries to the car for a young mother juggling bags and baby. Even glancing over your shoulder to check if you need to hold the door for someone behind you demonstrates caring.
- Extend common courtesies to family members by saying, "Please," "Thank you," and, "You're welcome." We say that to our friends, so why not to our family?

In order to show caring and compassionate behavior to others, children need to experience people caring about *them*. One mother, growing up in a home where verbal abuse was common, gave little thought to caring for others. Her main focus revolved around her own self-preservation. Only after getting involved in a church youth group did she have a sense of being cared for. Today, as a happily married mother of two, she makes a continuous effort to show her family she cares. Her hope is that after experiencing compassionate behavior, her children will demonstrate that same compassion.

The Character Education Partnership offers free information on a variety of character education programs. 1-800-988-8081.
A Call to Character: A Family Treasury by Colin Greer and Herbert Kohl, HarperCollins.

Winter Barbecues

"Demonstrate Christianity at all times and if necessary use words."   St. Francis of Assisi

During a severe winter snowstorm, our community suffered electrical outages. An appeal came over our portable radio requesting blankets for a local nursing home. Although warm and snug in front of our fireplace, we decided this was a perfect opportunity to help others. So at 9:00 P.M. we drove over icy roads to deliver seven blankets to the grateful residents. Our fourteen-year-old daughter saw firsthand how helping others requires effort yet produces positive results. Driving home she remarked, "It feels good to know I could help those people get warm even though I got cold walking through the parking lot."

After a few more minutes of quiet reflection, she added in typical teenage fashion, "I'm hungry! I wish I had a steak." Her ever-spontaneous father stopped at a store and purchased a steak. Then, at 10:00 P.M. on the coldest night of the year, they proceeded to barbecue steak on the front porch while singing summer camp songs. I, however, preferred reading a good book on the couch with my St. Bernard warming my feet.

Raising creative and caring children means taking action when opportunities arise. Here are some ideas for doing that:

- One family performed a secret good deed once a month. Activities ranged from washing the pastor's car to delivering homemade bread to a new mother. On one occasion, the family waited until an elderly neighbor went for a doctor's visit. Then they sprang quickly into action with Dad mowing her lawn, Mom trimming her bushes, and kids planting colorful flowers. Part of the fun was getting the task completed before the neighbor returned.

- Let children see you offer help before it is asked. If your church announces an upcoming missionary conference, Vacation Bible School, or teen sports night, call and see how your family can be involved.

- When you pull into a grocery store parking lot, return a stray shopping cart or two that someone carelessly left behind.

> "From now on in America, any definition of a successful life must include others."   George Bush

Writing for Any Reason

Where would we be without the written word? So much of Jesus' life would be unknown if people hadn't written letters and documented events. Numerous possibilities exist to foster creativity through writing.

- Give each child a journal in which to record thoughts and experiences. Keep a journal yourself and let your children see you writing in it. Even children too young to write can keep a journal. They can record their activities and accomplishments by drawing in their journals.

- Work together to create a family newsletter. Describe a silly event or future vacation plan. Share results of report cards, lost teeth, and work promotions. Send the newsletter to relatives or just keep it long-term as a document about family activities.

- Have children write their own books. Many computer programs come with templates for stories and pictures. Handwritten books are very special, since it's nice to have a record of the progression of handwriting skills.

- Enter contests. Many Sunday newspaper supplements carry rules for contests sponsored by major corporations. These involve writing limericks or describing in fifty words or less why your family is creative. A good resource is *All the Best Contests for Kids* by Joan Bergstrom (Ten Speed Press), describing hundreds of contests. If you win an all-expense-paid trip to Hawaii, send me a postcard!

- With your family, write a poem about a special event or person. It doesn't have to have perfect iambic pentameter or even rhyme, as long as you have fun writing it. For the first ten years of our marriage, my husband and I would take turns giving each other a poem on our anniversary, summarizing the year's events. These are framed and hang on our wall as a reminder of our love for each other.

> Encourage writing with *My Journal: A Place to Write About God and Me* by Janet Knight and Lyn Gilliam, Upper Room Books.

Caught in the Act of Kindness

For the past several years, the media has made reference to *Random Acts of Kindness* by Conari Press. The book details numerous people affected by acts of kindness. While such acts are wonderful, I can't help thinking about the numerous acts of kindness Jesus performed on a daily basis. He healed the twelve-year-old girl, fed hungry people, and spoke to people labeled "outcasts."

Our children need the opportunity to observe and participate in acts of kindness. We *talk* about donating food to the food bank, but do we actually do it? Do our children have any idea why we give away food and why it is even needed? It's all too easy to grab some cans off our pantry shelf and drop them in the food collection box at church or in a supermarket bin set up for that purpose. It's much more difficult to go to the food bank ourselves and distribute the food.

One family with an eight and twelve year old set a goal of doing one planned act of kindness each month. At times it was as simple as sending part of their allowance to a local zoo. Other times they spent several hours picking up litter. While the once-a-month activity seemed structured, it introduced children to the act of caring and giving.

Some other ways to spread random acts of kindness:

- Donate your children's old, but clean, books to a low-income preschool.
- Have your family help a shut-in decorate for the holidays.
- Send thank you cards to teachers, pastors, and librarians.
- Set up a bird feeder at a nursing home for the residents to watch. Maintain a relationship with the residents by visiting them and refilling the bird feeders on a regular basis.
- Sponsor a child overseas through a Christian organization.
- Give someone a compliment.
- Offer to check and replace the batteries in an elderly person's smoke detector.
- If a neighbor is ill, offer to take his or her dog for a walk.
- When classmates or friends get their picture in the paper, cut it out and give them the extra copy.

Waiting With Grace

Americans don't like to wait. We are fretful at red lights, antsy in long check out lines, and irritated at slow waiters. Even a thirty-second delay finds us mumbling about poor service.

Southwest Airlines knows people dislike waiting if a flight is delayed. To help passengers get through the waiting time, ticket agents carry a game book of easy-to-do activities that they hand out when people are delayed. Sometimes they sponsor a trivia contest or ask people to sing over the microphone. Sometimes they ask people to produce their driver's license pictures. The person with the ugliest photo wins a prize!

Wouldn't it be a good idea for us, as parents, to have our own game plan for times when our children have to wait? Here are some ideas to pass time:

- Carry this book with you as a handy reference guide for quick activities.
- Take turns closing your eyes while someone asks questions such as: "What color are the walls in this room?" "What kind of shoes am I wearing?" "Describe the carpet in this room."
- Hand someone a pencil and paper. Ask the person to close his or her eyes and draw something silly such as "a dog wearing a tutu" or "a tree with candy for leaves."
- Make up an exaggerated story about why you have to wait. Could it be that the cook had to run to the dairy to milk the cow in order to cook your pancakes? Maybe the dentist is late because she got invited to go bungee jumping with her daughter and is now dangling by her feet over a river filled with crocodiles.

Rather than complaining about the wait, enjoy the opportunity to be together. Don't whine—just use the few minutes for games and fun.

"Patience is the ability to idle your motor when you feel like stripping your gears."   Barbara Johnson

Creativity Enhancers

Teresa Amabile, a psychology professor and author of *Growing Up Creative: Nurturing a Lifetime of Creativity* (Crown Publishers), states: "Encouraging creative thinking in children prepares them for lifelong problem solving."

Isn't that what we want in our children? The ability to work through and solve problems instead of giving up in despair or going along with the crowd? In order to give children the ability to solve problems, they need a strong foundation of creative thinking. Try these ideas:

- Use open-ended questions as often as possible. A closed question is "Samantha, should you hit your brother when he takes your crayons?" The child will obviously answer "no." An open-ended question such as "Samantha, instead of hitting your brother, what could you do when Jeff grabs your crayons?" allows her room for creative thought.

- Try not to evaluate every idea your child offers. Doing so gives the child a feeling of being judged or critiqued. If a child has an idea for a new hairstyle or an innovative method of doing chores, let him or her try it out (keeping safety considerations in mind, of course).

- Encourage children to do something for the personal satisfaction of accomplishing a task. If children are doing their tasks only to get your approval, they will be more likely to follow the tried and true, acceptable method rather than finding creative approaches.

- Let your child know it's OK to make mistakes. One five year old, whose parents were very strict about any form of messiness, refused to use the bottle of glue for a Sunday school project. "I might spill glue on the table, so I'm not going to do the craft," he told his teacher. Let children see we all learn by taking risks, making mistakes, and spilling the glue.

> "Do not go where the path may lead, go instead where there is no path and then leave a trail."
> Ralph Waldo Emerson

The Printed Word

Over and over parents are told, "Read to your children." Student test scores continue to drop in the area of reading and comprehension. School districts are so concerned that they now hire reading specialists to help out. Some children could be greatly helped by parents reading to them.

Teach your children the wonder of the printed word. Show them it is a marvelous way to visit other children in a foreign land or to walk where Jesus walked. Show them how reading can expand their world. In addition to reading to your child, try some of the following activities to help make the printed word come alive:

- Give your child a phone book and ask fun questions, such as: "Who could I call if I wanted to build an Olympic-sized swimming pool in the backyard?" or "Let's pretend we have a horse that needs a new saddle. Who could I call to get that information?" Children learn that reading is the key to valuable information.

- Have your child put labels on various objects in the house. Friends may chuckle at seeing the front door labeled "door" and signs on items such as "Dad's chair" and "garbage can," but the labels help children associate printed words with actual items. (Don't forget to wear a "Mom" or "Dad" sign on your forehead!)

- Prepare a menu that has more than one option. Let children read it and check off their choices. They can choose from milk or juice, ice cream or Jell-O, and so forth.

- When going on a trip, even for a short distance, encourage children to read a map. Can they follow directions and find a new route to get to school or to the store?

- One mother, knowing her children often read cereal boxes during breakfast, wrote Bible memory verses and taped them to the back of cereal boxes.

> For a wonderful catalog of books for all ages, order *The Chinaberry Catalog*, 2780 Via Orange Way, Suite B, Spring Valley, CA 91978, 1-800-776-2242. Great bedtime reading.

Responding With "Yes!"

In order for children to feel safe enough to express creativity, adults must foster an atmosphere of trust and acceptance. Our natural reaction is to tell children, "That won't work," or, "You're too young to do that."

When conducting workshops on creativity for business groups, I attach "negative" strips to a few handouts. Then I ask for suggestions on how to improve one aspect of a job. People with the "negative strips" read out typical responses we give when people suggest a new idea. Do these sound familiar?

- It can't be done!
- We tried that before.
- It's too much work.
- Not that again!
- We're too busy.
- Where'd you dig up that idea?
- Good thought, but impractical.

It's no wonder businesses complain about employee apathy and lack of innovative ideas. But we have a wonderful opportunity to control the positive-negative environment in our homes. When a child offers a suggestion or introduces an idea, we can encourage creativity rather than squashing it. The first attempt to kick a soccer ball, sew a dress, or build a fort should be met with words of encouragement and hope. How about using these phrases?

- That's an original idea.
- Tell me more about your plan.
- Is there some way I can help?
- Sounds like you've really given this some thought.
- What a clever way to solve that problem.

When Jesus responded to others' ideas, his responses left them feeling valued and respected. Watch a child's face light up with wonder and excitement as you say, "Yes! I'll help you build a rope swing. Tell me what supplies we'll need."

Demonstrating Joy

Mother Teresa said, "Joy shows from your eyes; it appears when one speaks and walks. When people find in your eyes that habitual happiness, they will understand that they are the beloved children of God." Do our children see joy in our eyes when they enter a room? Do they feel the love of God through us?

Several years ago a great deal of publicity was generated about the way children in Romanian orphanages were being treated. The media showed pictures of solemn babies and toddlers peering up from cribs where they were confined all day long with very little human contact. But one magazine article showed a photo of a thin but smiling and alert sixteen-month-old baby. Abandoned by her parents, she, too, had only a few overworked childcare providers to look after her basic needs. The difference was that one doctor had developed a special affection for this little girl and visited her daily. When he came into her sterile room she'd clap her hands and bounce with joy. The next photo showed the same toddler at twenty months. Now she was unsmiling, thinner than before, and crouched in the corner of her crib. Her beloved doctor had been transferred to another city and could no longer visit her. As he held the baby for the last time, he told a news reporter, "Every child needs to have someone in his life whose face lights up when he sees that child."

Think about your favorite teacher. More than likely his or her face lit up when you entered the room.

Here are some specific ways to demonstrate joy:

- Make a conscious effort to let your child see joy in your eyes when he or she enters a room.
- Even if just going to the neighborhood store for milk, ask one of your children to go along.
- If you are away from home for more than a day, phone or e-mail each child individually.
- Give your child small pats or hugs on a casual basis. We have a tradition in our house that if Sondra is going up the stairs ahead of me, I try to catch her and kiss her belly button.
- Most of all, say "I love you" to your child daily.

> *Bringing Out the Best in Your Child* by Cynthia
> Tobias and Carol Funk, Servant Publications.
> *Do You Know What I Like About You?* by Cynthia
> Tobias, Servant Publications.

Reading After College

As you probably know, Oprah Winfrey started a once-a-month book club on her television show. She simply shares a favorite book and then asks viewers to read the book. The results amazed even her. Thousands of people wrote with comments about books they had read. Most astonishing was the large number of people who wrote, "I haven't read a book since I graduated from college, but you inspired me to get into the reading habit again."

We read to our children, and we encourage them to read, but are we reading too? Here are some ways to encourage family reading:

- Make a large paper outline of a tree and attach it to a door or wall. Have children cut out leaf shapes and keep them next to the tree. Whenever someone reads a book, record that person's name and title of the book on a leaf. Glue the leaf on a paper tree limb. Then you can all watch the family reading tree flourish as family members read more.

- Purchase a guest book and have visitors sign it when they visit your house. Ask guests to write down the title of a favorite book along with their names.

- Next time you have a get-together at your house, post several large sheets of paper on the wall with headings such as "Best Adult Nonfiction Book I've Read," "My Preschooler's Favorite Books," or "Best Novel I've Read." Encourage people to fill in their choices. It's a great way for everyone to get new ideas on book selections.

- Many families encourage reading by allowing children to stay up past their bedtime if they read in bed.

- Make a paper chain recording how many books your family reads. As soon as a book is completed, write the title on a strip of paper and add it to the chain. Hopefully, it will be long enough to drape throughout your house.

- When reading about distant locations, get an atlas and pinpoint where the event takes place.

A recent study showed 58 percent of the American public never read a book again after high school.

Doing Things Together

Fifteen hundred children participated in a questionnaire entitled "Secrets of Strong Families." When asked, "What do you think makes a happy family?" how do you think they responded? It wasn't taking weekly trips to Disneyland or eating out three times a week. It was "Doing things together." Working and playing together was the most important element in building a happy family.

Even with busy schedules, it is possible to do things as a family in a relaxed and fun atmosphere and to incorporate your needs and desires into your children's daily life. One mother looked forward to reading the newspaper in the evening but found she ended up dozing off after the second page. Now, every night after dinner, she sets the timer for twenty minutes. Everyone gathers in the living room and reads quietly until the buzzer sounds. That's not very exciting, but at a parent-teacher conference, the teacher told the parents their son had said the best part of his day is sitting next to Dad while they both read.

Doing things together can't be forced. Demanding your child accompany you on a walk only fosters resentment. However, going on a walk and getting a piggyback ride, or stopping to look at the neighbor's puppies, makes a walk a joyful experience. When Trina was a teenager, she and her dad would take trips to the dump. They both enjoyed the scenic country ride between home and the dump. After they had unloaded the trash, Trina would practice her driving in the middle of a deserted field.

To increase your time together:

- Ask younger children if they want you to read to them as they bathe.
- Sit next to your child and pay bills or write letters while he or she does homework.
- Offer to assist your child in cleaning a bedroom. Refrain from giving directions.
- Take your child to breakfast on a school morning.
- If appropriate, take your child to work for a few hours. Better yet, take the child along on a business trip. Most hotels offer an approved list of baby-sitters to watch children while parents attend to business. This is a wonderful way of gaining valuable time with your child even though you are traveling.

Tithing Your Time

A family that had always been very active in and supportive of their local church faced financial difficulties. Unable to give a full tithe, they scheduled a family meeting to discuss the situation. After tossing around a few ideas, they decided to tithe their time and talents until their finances stabilized.

A quick call to the church resulted in a list of short-term projects. For several months, they donated two hours of work to the church each Monday evening. Everyone participated, even the six year old. On one occasion, her job consisted of sorting out a large box of colored markers from Sunday school classes and discarding the ones that were no longer useable. Other family members cleaned storage closets, wiped down folding chairs and repaired broken nursery toys, dusted library bookshelves and created a display of lost and found items. One sunny evening found them weeding the flower beds around the church.

We often hand children money to put it in the offering plate. The result is they often have little understanding about tithing. Tithing time and talents teaches children the importance of giving back to God the blessings he's given us. It's easier to write a check than to do physical work. Yet the work has to be done, too. And in those circumstances where we are unable to give financially, we can model to our children the value of giving in other ways. Some ideas include:

- Call shelters or other Christian ministries to see what their current needs are.
- Sponsor a garage sale and donate a portion (or all) of the proceeds to church.

- Serve meals at a homeless shelter on a regular basis.
- Think creatively. One family heard about a need for Bibles. They gathered Bibles left in several churches' lost and found boxes and shipped them to China.

Cleaning Out the Toy Box

How many Barbie dolls are in your house? How many stuffed animals? Are there more than ten? Do toy boxes spill over with toys that seldom see the light of day? In all likelihood, just part of your children's toys are more than some children see in a year. Birthdays, holidays, and even graduation from kindergarten provoke a gift-giving frenzy. When children outgrow toys or have duplicates, look for creative ways to recycle them:

- Together with your children, collect *all* their toys and place them in the center of a room. (Make sure you have an hour or so to complete this job).
- Ask children to make a quick evaluation of the toys they want and those they don't. Have them put all the unwanted ones into a box.
- Have children select from the remaining toys their all-time favorites. Put those back on the shelves or in the toy boxes.
- The pile that's left are toys that fall into the "so-so" category. These items get occasional use but wouldn't be missed too much if they were gone. If children can't be convinced to donate them, put all the toys in storage where they can be found if they are really wanted. Store them for a few months, and after that time have the children reevaluate what to do with the toys.

- Go through your first box of discarded toys. If some are in good condition, donate them to a group home or shelter. Now get ruthless and throw out all the broken cars, dolls with missing heads, and chewed-up puzzle pieces.

Cleaning and sorting toys not only makes for a neater house, it encourages children to take inventory of their items. One mother put all her children's toys in a guest room and locked the door. For twenty-four hours, the house was "toy-free" and her children gained a new appreciation for what they had.

Through Sickness and Health

It's easy to be playful and carry out creative activities when you are rested and your children are in a good mood. But there are those times when you've been up all night with a sick child.

When illness hits a family, this, too is time to get creative. Anyone can attempt to comfort a sick child with one video after another, but it takes extra effort to find ways to pass the time, especially if a child has to stay in bed for a period of time.

Children learn compassion for others if they receive compassion from you. One mother, tired from caring for her young son with the flu, fell asleep midday while reading him a book. Her ten-year-old daughter, seeing the situation, covered her mom with a blanket and then carried her younger brother to bed, where she continued to read the story. Later, she told her mother, "You always take care of *me* when I'm sick, so I wanted to take care of Brandon."

Here are some other ways to provide physical and psychological comfort:

- Make cassette tapes of the healthy family members singing, telling jokes, and reading stories for the sick child.
- Give your child a bell or a musical instrument to use to call you. (This is easier on your nerves also.)
- If a child is bedridden for a long time, periodically move him or her to your bed or to a sibling's room. A change of scenery is a welcome relief to a bored child.

Creative Caring

The Bible tells us when one part of the body suffers, the rest of the body is affected also. When a family member is ill, often the usual family dynamics are altered. (Especially if Mom is sick!) This is the time to rally together with, "What can we do to help Alison while she has a fever and needs to stay in bed?" Younger children can draw cards or pictures while older siblings contribute by reading stories or making paper dolls. When a six year old was contagious with chicken pox, his four-year-old twin sisters stood outside his bedroom window, making faces. They'd stand at the side of the window, pop out, make a goofy face, and then disappear to the opposite side of the window. The object was to make their silliest faces while their brother tried not to smile. At night their dad went into the sickroom and used a flashlight to create shadow figures on the wall. (*Shadowgraphs Anyone Can Make* by Phila Webb and Jose Corby, Running Press, gives directions on making thirty different shadows.)

- Put a spring-tension rod in the door frame, and drop a beach towel over it, creating an instant puppet stage. The sick child rests in bed, enjoying spontaneous puppet shows from anyone walking by his or her doorway.

- Try serving a small amount of food in muffin tins. An assortment of finger foods placed in the individual spaces makes food appealing. Prepare a variety of juices or milkshakes and serve with a straw. Your child may still be grumpy and probably spill the juice, but the message you convey remains the same—"I care about you."

- If you really want to "lighten" the situation, bring several tree branches into the sick child's room. Decorate the branches with small white Christmas lights for an instant fairy tale effect.

The National Association for the Education of Young Children offers a helpful booklet with guidelines about when a child should stay home from school.
Request #706 $2.00
1509-16th St. NW, Washington, DC 20036.

TV or Not TV?

The decision to subscribe to cable TV was simple for us. Due to the remote location of our house, it would cost $16,000 for the privilege of watching television! We decided to try a satellite dish after seeing an inexpensive one for sale in the newspaper. We had great reception for one day—until our sheep discovered the huge dish made a great back-rubbing post. They'd move their massive bodies against the metal dish and disturb the alignment needed for clear reception. We put down the TV guide and picked up books and games instead.

The amount of TV your family watches is a personal issue. In 1984, a Connecticut librarian initiated a month-long, town-wide TV Turn-Off. The event received national publicity and generated similar programs around the country. It's estimated four million people participated in the 1996 event and turned off their TVs for a month.

If you don't want to get that drastic, at least try the following ideas to put *you* back in control of the TV:

- Watch TV *with* your child. Some programs you think are suitable take on new meaning when you actually watch them.

- Put the mute on during commercials. Point out to children how advertisers try to make the products look fast, colorful, and exciting.

- Select programs in advance. Make the selections together as a family. Then, turn on the TV at the beginning of the program and turn it off at the end—no staying around to catch the first part of the next show.

- Discuss real life and acting. Can people *truly* crash cars and remain uninjured?

- Point out how people often are portrayed in stereotypes. Girls always complain about math problems, and low-income people are always on drugs.

- Ask your child questions about the show. "Why did the boy skip school? Was there another way to avoid fighting?"

- Express your views about the characters in a nonjudgmental way.

One mother cut down on TV viewing time by replacing their large color television with a small black-and-white unit!

More persons have television (99 percent) in their homes than indoor plumbing.

Digging Out of the Rut

We all need a certain amount of routine to provide consistency and stability to our lives. But there's a big difference between beneficial routines and being in a rut. A routine that builds security is having dinner together as a family. Eating meat loaf and mashed potatoes seven days a week is more routine than anyone needs—it's a rut. To avoid getting into a rut:

- Assign family members to make one change somewhere in the house on a daily basis. See if others can guess what's different.
- From time to time, purchase potpourri and produce a new fragrance in your home. Have family members try to guess what the potpourri is called.
- Gather the family and in fifteen minutes rearrange the living room furniture. Even if you don't like the way it turned out, try the new arrangement for a few days.
- Purchase colored light bulbs and see how the atmosphere changes with pink lights in the bathroom and a green glow in the kitchen.
- To avoid the gloominess of a long dark winter, one family kept their Christmas lights up in the living room from December to March.
- Serve dessert first at dinner.

- Just before bedtime, wear your pajamas—that includes *you*—load everyone into the car and go to a drive-thru restaurant for ice cream cones.
- Leave small gifts or notes in unexpected places. One father delivered a small bouquet of flowers to his daughter at her dance class. The whole studio shared in an obvious expression of love between father and daughter.
- Do something creative for family devotions. Invite neighbors over or act out Bible stories.
- Try a sunrise breakfast. Gather muffins, juice, and fruit the night before. Check the paper for local sunrise time, and get up early enough to catch the sun coming over the horizon.

> *The Bible Ride: Adventures that Bring the Gospel to Life* (in three volumes) by Gary Moon (Servant Publications) offers relevant, fun, and interesting devotions based on the life of Christ.

Object Lessons at Home

During a recent Sunday service, our pastor asked for prayer requests. A few people briefly requested prayer for better health, for relatives to be saved, and to find employment. Then a regular church member stood up to gain the pastor's attention. This young man had Down Syndrome and spoke in a slow, halting manner, making it difficult to understand his thoughts. He spoke for a long time and gave many details about his prayer request. People began fidgeting and showing signs of restlessness as he continued to speak. I watched our pastor the entire time. He listened with full eye contact, never shuffling or trying to shorten the young man's comments. Later, as Pastor Brad began his sermon on patience, I knew I had just witnessed patience in action.

It seems so trite to tell our children, "Actions speak louder than words" when we don't take responsibility for our own actions. Children need visual cues and solid examples to understand what we are trying to teach them. We might tell our children to allow God to direct their lives, but they have little understanding of what that means. Many children's sermons use object lessons, so why not try a few at home?

- Cut a straw in half. String it over a piece of fish line or waxed dental floss which is then strung across the room. Blow up a balloon and hold the end shut as you tape the balloon to the straw. Explain to your child how God wants to direct our lives. Let go of the balloon end and it should shoot across the room on the line. (You might want to practice a bit before you use this as an object lesson.) Now blow up a balloon and release it. Watch how it spins and sputters randomly, similar to our lives without God.

- Blow a few bubbles. Point out to children how quickly they pop. The things we have on earth are temporary, but our life with Jesus is eternal.

- Make fingerprints of your children by putting their fingers on an ink pad and then on a plain piece of paper. Describe to children how our fingerprints change everything we touch. Then talk with them about how their lives touch other students and teachers at school. We leave our "mark" through words and actions.

> *Making Memories That Count: Nurturing Your Child in Christian Values* by Debra Fulghum Bruce, Gospel Publishing House.
>
> *Easy to Use Object Lessons* by Sheryl Bruinsma, Baker Book House.

School Bells

In our community, home-schooled children maintain a high profile. They sponsor bazaars, conduct community service projects, and join sports programs. Home-school parents are actively supporting and enhancing their children's learning. Whether your children attend private school, are home-schooled, or go to the local public school, many possibilities exist to further their education. This doesn't mean an endless round of flashcards or worksheets before breakfast.

It does mean:

- Find a way to volunteer in your child's classroom. Studies show children do better in school when parents take an active interest in school activities. Due to my speaking schedule, I have difficulty being a classroom assistant on a regular basis. So when the teacher asked for a six-by-nine-foot reading carpet, I knew that was something I could contribute to the classroom. From time to time I send in special supplies for craft projects, and once I even coaxed our pet sheep into the car for a trip to school and a lesson on sheep.

- Don't overschedule children with so many activities that they go to school weary.
- Keep teachers informed about major events in your family, such as the death of a pet or job changes.
- Ask to see your child's school records. Request the principal to clarify any unusual statements.
- Have books and magazines available throughout your house to stimulate your child's interest and creativity.
- Review your child's homework on a regular basis.
- Let children see you use resources such as maps and dictionaries to find answers to your questions.
- Create a quiet space for homework with good lighting and few distractions.
- Limit TV and video games.

Children spend the majority of their day at school. When you think about it, it makes sense to be a part of their experience in the classroom. Schools are limited in what they teach and the amount of time they can give to it. As parents we have a vested interest to elaborate, discover, and enjoy teaching our children.

For a variety of educational and noncommercial children's products, order the free Animal Town catalog, 1-800-445-8642.

Just Because You're Special

Proverbs 15:13 tells us: "A joyful heart makes a cheerful face." There comes a time in every family when one member doesn't have a joyful heart and needs some cheering up. Here are a few ways to let that person know he or she is a special part of your family:

- Cut toast into special shapes with cookie cutters. If you have alphabet cookie cutters, spell out an "I love you" sign from the toast.
- Draw a picture of your house. In the windows, glue a picture of each family member. Label the picture, "This house is filled with love," or some other appropriate caption.
- Buy the person a mylar balloon and deliver it to work or school.
- Purchase or make a simple, plain-colored pillow. Have family members autograph the pillow with permanent markers and add personal messages. Put it on the recipient's bed at night.

A home that is based on God's teachings is the best place to teach children love and compassion. Rather than saying, "Don't be noisy, Mom had a hard day at work and has a headache," take a few minutes to discuss ways of helping Mom. Perhaps Dad makes sandwiches for dinner and everyone goes on a walk while Mom reads a book in peace and quiet. Collect colorful leaves or wildflowers and bring Mom home a bouquet of love.

The concept of creative family living goes beyond arts and crafts projects and celebrating the hamster's birthday. It takes place in the quick moments of jotting a note of appreciation to a teacher, setting the table with the "fancy" china, or trying a new recipe.

One family frequently practices what they call "ten minutes of caring." Someone sets the timer for ten minutes. During that time family members scurry around, attempting to perform an act of caring. Adults might call a distant friend or write a letter. Children draw a picture for Grandma, vacuum the car, or empty the dishwasher without being asked. Everyone experiences the feeling of doing something nice for someone else.

The Art of Fine Conversation

Does your family sit around the dinner table at night, discussing the latest political campaign or summarizing Sunday's sermon? Or do you barely get through two bites of food before someone tells a gross joke or calls a brother an "imbecile"?

Teaching children the art of conversation involves modeling, practice, and patience. Remember how excited we were when our grinning baby said "Dada"? A child spoke, we listened, we clapped, we cheered. Then when our children evolved into highly verbal beings, we asked them to be quiet or to get to the point of their stories.

If you were talking to your best friend, would you interrupt with, "Oh, it's not so bad—everyone goes through that"? If they told you about a problem, would you respond by saying, "That wasn't a smart way to handle the situation"? Of course you wouldn't. Yet we interrupt our children and stunt conversation with canned responses.

Here are some suggestions for raising the level of conversation when dealing with children:

- Take time to listen. A cry of "Nobody likes me" doesn't require an automatic response from you. Wait, listen, and wait some more. Your actions teach children to attentively listen to others.

- Talk *with* your child rather than *at* your child. Put the paper down, stop folding clothes, and make eye contact with your child.

- If you absolutely can't stop to listen to your child, write a note stating when you *will* be able to listen. Seeing "Mom and Jordan will meet tonight at 7:00 P.M. to discuss his science experiment" posted on the refrigerator shows your child the importance of communication.

- Let children see you engaging in adult conversation. Invite them to stay and quietly listen or leave the room, but do not let them interrupt. Stress that this is a time for adults to share their thoughts and ideas.

- Ask interesting questions. A routine question like "Did you have a good day?" gets a routine answer. Interesting questions produce interesting responses.

How to Have Intelligent and Creative Conversations with Your Kids by Dr. Jane Healy, Doubleday.

Kid Talk: Small Talk! Big Fun!: Great Conversation Starters With Kids are cards designed to stimulate discussions. Published by Table Talk.

"X" Marks the Spot

J esus gave many examples about the treasures awaiting Christians. Matthew 13:44 states, "The kingdom of heaven is like a treasure hidden in the field." Spend a few minutes discussing the everyday "treasures" God gives us in the form of friends, food, and health. Ask your children if they want to go on a treasure hunt. (Why would they say no?) Here's how to conduct a treasure hunt:

- Before the treasure hunt, hide a treasure. A bag of gold chocolate coins is always fun.
- Cut open a large, brown paper grocery bag. Use it to draw the treasure map. For added authenticity, crumple and unroll the paper several times. Singe the edges with a flame to create a realistic-looking old map.
- Sketch out the general treasure area—it can be as large as your neighborhood or as small as a single room. This narrows down the places where your children will search.
- Color the map, labeling a few areas children might have difficulty locating.
- Include a list of instructions such as: "Begin by our black trash can. Walk three giant steps forward, turn to the left and find a round rock. Lift it up for the next clue."
- Under the rock place another clue such as: "Find the doghouse on your map. Check the tree directly behind it." Naturally you've hidden another clue in the tree.
- When children get to the last clue, instruct them to dig in the dirt. Hopefully their search will have led them to the treasure—a bag of gold chocolate coins or other treasure you have hidden.

One mother set up a treasure hunt that included a Bible verse to correspond with each clue. She concluded the activity with snacks and a chance to discuss how God leads us from one area of our lives to another.

I'll Be Your Waiter This Evening

A letter to the editor in a recent magazine complained about parents bringing young children to an elegant five-star restaurant. For most of us, the only five-stars we see in restaurants is in a design our child draws on a paper placemat at an all-you-can-eat buffet. Eating out can be expensive, so why not invite your children to manage their own restaurant for the evening?

- Help children brainstorm the theme and name of their restaurant. Will it have a Mexican decor? Are reservations required? Do guests need to dress up?
- Let children pick the menu and cook as much of the meal as possible. One mother of three children paid a college student to come over for two hours to assist with restaurant set-up and meal preparation. This meant Mom and Dad had two glorious hours of uninterrupted time, and the children were able to keep the meal a complete secret from their parents.
- When planning the special meal, suggest to your children ways to create atmosphere. Background music and decorated napkins add to a theme. A centerpiece or painting for the wall could reflect the restaurant's decor.
- When it's time to eat, have children dress like waiters and take your order. Just watch out. They may hand you a steep bill at the end of the meal.

Children enjoy running a pretend restaurant and serving you. Once in a while, turn the tables and create a special restaurant for your children. Keep the kitchen off-limits while you are getting ready so they can't see how you've transformed an ordinary dining table into a Hawaiian feast or a country-western steak-house.

As you leave your fancy at-home restaurant, be sure to leave your cheerful staff a tip!

Learning the Work Ethic

"**M**om, can I have seventy-five dollars for a new pair of shoes?" That question creates an instant desire to deliver "Parents' Lecture Number Three."

"When I was your age, I had cardboard in my shoes because the soles were so thin," you tell them. "Do you have any idea how hard I work to earn seventy-five dollars?" The next time your children need extra cash, offer to help them develop money-making plans beyond the traditional lemonade stand.

Some parents post a "jobs available" sheet listing additional household chores and the price offered for those chores. While putting away the lawn furniture for the summer isn't a glamorous job, it is something one of your children might do for a reasonable rate. List the chores that need doing but never seem to get completed. When Trina was ten, I paid her one dollar to straighten out my sewing chest. She spent more than an hour neatly rewinding thread on the spools and organizing the odds and ends of needles and buttons.

- One enterprising first-grader found a job. He played with the neighbor's two-year-old son for half an hour, twice a week. The grateful mother stayed in the same room, of course, but was able to catch up on a few projects as the children played.

- Two eleven year olds, who liked riding bikes, developed a unique business of taking *down* garage sale signs. After a long day of conducting garage sales, people were all too glad to pay the boys to remove the signs from telephone poles.

Naturally, children should help out at home with everyday chores on a regular basis. So before they venture out on money-raising jobs, remind them about the importance of completing their regular chores around the house.

> "Kids in the Marketplace," a five-part leaflet series offering parents advice for teaching children important financial/consumer concepts and skills, is available for $6 from the Cornell University Resource Center, 7BTP, Ithaca, NY 14850.

Cash for Kids

As children develop ways to earn money, try to achieve a balance of spending and saving. Tithing—giving 10 percent to the Lord's work—takes on new meaning when a child puts his or her hard-earned money in the collection plate. One practical-minded eleven year old earned twenty-five dollars running a mini-carnival in her backyard. Before depositing her tithe of two dollars and fifty cents, she asked the pastor how her money would be spent. She didn't want her money being wasted!

Still looking for ways to help children earn money? Here are some:

- Older children could teach lessons on French braiding hair to younger girls.

- Contact neighbors to walk their dogs. If you don't trust your children to walk neighbors' dogs around the block, they could exercise them in a fenced yard. Throwing sticks or Frisbees and chasing each other provide exercise for both the dog and the child.

- How about a door-to-door car wash? Children arrive on a neighbor's doorsteps with rags, buckets, and window spray, offering a personalized car wash.

- Older children make great parent-helpers at children's birthday parties. Parents are grateful for an extra person to serve cake and control chaos. Truly ambitious children with specific skills can offer to perform magic tricks, lead singing, or teach a craft to the happy birthday group. A skilled twelve-year-old soccer player made a good source of income by going to parties and conducting a twenty-minute mini soccer clinic. Children looked up to the "older" coach, and parents appreciated having the children let off steam, running and kicking the ball in a productive way.

101 Marvelous Money-Making Ideas for Kids by Heather Wood, Tor Books.

The Lemonade Stand by Emmanuel Modu, Gateway Publishing.

Distributing $10,000

S tatistics show the majority of people are late in planning for retirement. While it's too early for your toddler to understand the stock market, there are ways to give children financial skills beyond using a plastic piggy bank:

- Take children to the bank and set up a savings account. (Call ahead and you might be able to arrange a tour of their vault and safety deposit box area.) Let children put their signatures on the passbook. When chunks of money come in for birthdays or graduations, help them decide how much to save and how much to spend. Discuss under what circumstances children may withdraw money from their account. Setting guidelines in advance avoids "Why can't I take out all my savings to buy twelve more video games?"

- The stock market remains a mystery to most people. (When you see the New York Stock Exchange on television, don't you wonder what all those people are yelling about?) Obtain a children's book giving the basics of stocks. Some companies let you purchase one share of their stock and then buy more stock when you have money to do so. Purchasing a stock gives children a feeling of ownership and begins to teach them about financial planning.

- If you don't want to actually invest money, set up a pretend account. Say that every family member has a pretend $10,000 to invest. Record which companies each person chooses. Check the newspapers on a regular basis and keep track of each person's portfolio to see if he or she has made a wise investment choice.

Saving money is a wise and necessary part of life. As you assist children in developing a savings plan, discuss the even greater importance of storing up our treasures in heaven. We can easily lose money in the stock market but can never lose the rewards God has awaiting us in heaven.

The Totally Awesome Money Book for Kids and Their Parents by Adriane Berg or *A Kid's Guide to Managing Money* by Joy Wilt, Children's Press.

The Young Investor's Fund is designed to introduce children to long-term investing. They receive posters, booklets, and information on companies that affect the lives of children. Phone: 1-800-403-0550.

Be Careful!

Think about the last time your child carried a plate of food to the table. "Be careful," you admonish. "You'll drop it." When your child says, "Mom, look at me on top of the jungle gym," you quickly call out, "Be careful. You'll fall."

Then when it is time for your child to audition for a solo in the Sunday school pageant, and she says, "I can't do it," you wonder why.

Biting your tongue to avoid saying "Be careful" is one of the most difficult aspects of parenting. It's just so natural! Giving children the opportunity to take age-appropriate risks increases their self-esteem. What preschoolers haven't beamed with delight because they "helped" wash the car? Sure, they're sopping wet, they spilled the bucket of soapy water, and they squirted you with the hose, but they accomplished a task. Think how that same experience is altered if you say, "Now, don't get wet, you'll catch a cold." "Be careful not to spill this bucket." "You'll be in time-out if you squirt me with the hose."

Have you ever been nervous when attempting to share your faith? There's a chance the person will laugh or ridicule your beliefs. Yet, if you've had success taking risks in the past, you're likely to feel confident enough to overcome the butterflies in your stomach. Building confidence obviously doesn't mean giving your preschooler a running chainsaw. But it does mean assisting your preschooler to use a handsaw to cut a thin piece of wood.

The next time you get the urge to say, "Be careful," try this instead:

- "Stay there. I want to get my camera and take a picture of you climbing that tree!"
- Give short, specific instructions. "Peel the potato away from your body." "Hold the railing when you climb stairs."
- Remain silent and observe your child for a few seconds before making any comment.

> "Our objective as parents ... is to do nothing for boys and girls which they can profit from doing themselves."   James Dobson

Gaining New Experiences

Children exposed to a wide variety of experiences grow up to be more interesting people. Their expanded frame of reference allows them to communicate about a variety of subjects with many different kinds of people. Think about the range of people Jesus dealt with. He ate among ranking rulers and then spoke with the woman at the well.

Some low-cost ways to help children gain new experiences include:

- Invite a visiting missionary for breakfast or a picnic. (Missionaries always get invited out for dinner.)

- Serve a new fruit or vegetable obtained from a gourmet store. None of you may like it, but the family will have a new taste experience.

- Next time you're in your usual shopping area, visit a few surrounding stores that are unfamiliar to you. Stop in at an Asian market or a specialty tea shop.

A recent article in the newspaper asked some teen-aged gang members why they stay with a gang. The most frequent answers were, "It's exciting," and, "It gives me something to do." The article went on to describe how the teens felt their life was boring and they never had any new experiences.

Excitement doesn't have to be riding an elephant on an expensive African safari. (Of course, that would be fun.) Excitement for children is touching a sea star for the first time or feeling the nervous anticipation before dancing in a recital. It's up to us as parents to give our children these new experiences. Money isn't always a factor since there are numerous free or low-cost programs such as All-Comers Track Meets, library concerts, and hiking trails. The important factor is providing children with positive experiences, so they don't need to look to gangs as a source of excitement. All too often when we hear about a new exhibit at the museum or read that a submarine is available for tours, we say, "I really should take the kids." Then, caught up in everyday events, we forget. Make it a priority to provide one new experience for your family per week.

> When was the last time you tried something new?
> Begin by listening to a different radio station
> or even sitting in a different place in church.

A New Version of Pay Television

Whenever I speak at parenting conferences, parents complain about the excessive amount of television and videos their children watch. It's surprising how many parents feel powerless to control their children's viewing habits. Other than the obvious solution of selling your television set(s) or banning all television during the school week, there are other solutions.

In trying to raise creative and curious children, we want them to think, to question, and to participate. What benefit do they receive from viewing *The Lion King* twelve times? Sitting aimlessly in front of the television promotes little action. A study by Dr. Steve Gortmaker at the Harvard School of Public Health found the odds of being overweight were 4.6 times greater for kids who watched more than five hours of television daily than for those who watched less than two hours.

A mother, wanting to teach her two children to make their own decisions concerning television, set up a new version of pay television. Every Sunday evening, each child received two dollars and fifty cents. Every time they wanted to watch a half hour of television or videos, they paid fifty cents each. To encourage quality viewing, Christian programs were offered at twenty-five cents per half hour.

This system gave her children freedom to make their own choices within approved guidelines.

Other ways to limit TV viewing:

- After watching a show, turn the TV off immediately.
- Set a rule that homework must be completed before the TV goes on.
- One mother said the TV could be turned on only if all the toys were picked up in the family room. Her children played outside rather than clean up!

> "There's no other activity, besides watching TV, where kids are inactive and consistently induced to eat high caloric foods."
>
> Dr. Steven Gortmaker,
> Harvard School of Public Health

Resumes for All

High school seniors spend hours agonizing over writing the perfect resume. Resumes play a vital role in summing up your accomplishments.

Why wait until you are under pressure to produce a resume? Plan a family activity to document each other's talents and achievements by writing a resume. Writing a resume provides valuable experience in organizing facts, listing dates, and letting others know about your skills.

If you are actually applying for a job, it's best to follow the standard formats shown in many resource books. However, for family resumes, list broad categories such as:

- Special hobbies
- Favorite activities at school or work
- Experience on the playground (or in the workplace)
- Special people in my life
- Volunteer activities

Perhaps your child is constantly in the shadows of a high-profile, popular older sibling. Putting together a resume shows your restrained child the very special qualities he or she has. Brainstorm positive qualities about each family member.

Your child's resume could include his or her skill at doing cart-wheels, memorizing Bible verses, feeding the dog consistently, and teaching Grandpa to use a computer. There's a sense of pride in seeing your accomplishments in print. One family updates individual resumes annually. They also type and print them on parchment paper to highlight their importance. Bring out the resumes on a yearly basis and check your progress. Can Jessica count past twenty-five yet? Has Brandon learned to rollerblade? Did you finish your book?

Resume Resources: What Color Is Your Parachute? by Richard Bolles, Ten Speed Press.

Resume Writing: A Comprehensive How-to-Do-It Guide by Burdett Bostwick, John Wiley & Sons.

Long-Term Projects

Many teachers complain about the short attention span of children today. Rapid-fire video games, thirty-second television commercials, and even snippets of conversation with parents contribute to inattentiveness.

Combine a sense of adventure with teaching children stick-to-it skills by planning long-term projects.

There are many ways to help children learn the value of working on a project or activity beyond fifteen minutes:

- Have your children estimate how many days it will take to put a large puzzle together if everyone works on it six and one-half minutes each day. Then stick to it. Find a time of day, set the timer for six and one-half minutes, and see how long until the puzzle is complete. Offer a small prize to the person who estimated closest to the actual time.

- Assign children projects such as making dessert every day for a week or taking the dog to obedience class on a regular basis.

- Older children could spend five minutes a day reading to their young sibling.

- Write letters to the major television networks expressing satisfaction (or disappointment) at the quality of television programming. Wait for a reply. Networks estimate one postcard represents the opinions of 1,000 viewers.

ABC-TV	CBS-TV	NBC-TV
2040 Avenue of the Stars	7800 Beverly Blvd.	3000 W. Alameda
Los Angeles, CA 90047	Los Angeles, CA 90036	Burbank, CA 91523

Long-term projects don't need to be complicated. The key is consistency so your children see the results of their continued effort. Perhaps they could make a chart and record the daily weather for several weeks. One family recorded the main point of their pastor's sermon on a monthly basis. Another family designated their eleven-year-old son to keep track of relatives' birthdays. His mother purchased a box of assorted birthday cards, and he proudly used a special calendar to send out timely birthday greetings.

Megaskills: How Families Can Help Children Succeed in School and Beyond by Dorothy Rich, Houghton Mifflin.

Learning to Learn: Ways to Nurture Your Child's Intelligence by Angela Brown Miller, Plenum Publishing.

Young Teen Explorers

If you have young teenagers, no one needs to tell you how difficult this stage of life can be for them. They still want to be children but feel they need to act more mature. Their bodies develop at different rates, so some are more physically mature than others. Some begin to question their Christian beliefs. It's also a time when they want more freedom but have difficulty living up to the responsibility.

When our oldest daughter was thirteen, she wanted a summer job to earn money for designer-label school clothes. Since she was too young for a steady job, we devised a plan for her to earn some money. We called it "Summer Exploration." Together we brainstormed a list of meaningful activities and "jobs" she could do such as:

- Volunteering at a nursing home, youth program, or day care center.
- Reading books on a new topic and telling the family about them.
- Writing letters to relatives.
- Giving time to the church such as helping in the nursery, office, or Sunday school.
- Planning a family activity such as a game night or picnic.
- Cooking meals and cleaning up afterwards.
- Writing down goals and plans for the future, sealing them in an envelope, and storing the envelope some place where it can be retrieved in five years.
- Spending time playing with or baby-sitting a younger child.
- Taking a class or workshop to learn a new skill such as water-skiing, bowling, or soccer.

We agreed upon an amount of money for each task performed. Trina, our daughter, had fourteen days to choose and complete five items from the list. At that point she'd receive half the money for her clothing. After a week's break, she was to complete another five items within fourteen days for the remainder of the money. In a structured and productive way, she earned her own money for school clothes.

Facing the Consequences

A plan for earning money for school clothes like our "Summer Exploration" sounds like a great idea, doesn't it? The only problem is enforcing the agreement. If a teen completed only four of the required five tasks during the first fourteen-day period, according to our written contract, he or she cannot receive the "salary" for that period. While a parent might be tempted to compromise the original agreement, it is important for the teen to experience the natural consequence of his or her actions. In the actual work world, employees are expected to complete their job assignments on time. While teens may grumble at the very thought of having to "work" for clothes money, they will be learning valuable job skills that will benefit them in the future.

Trina struggled to complete her first fourteen-day assignment, but guess what happened during the next fourteen-day session? You're right! She completed all her required five tasks and proudly received her "salary" for that time period.

The idea worked so well, we continued the "Summer Exploration" for three more years.

By having your children participate in a "Summer Exploration" experience, they:

- gain a strong work ethic,
- develop a sense of control over finances, and
- meet interesting people and gain new experiences.

Employers today moan about the "twenty-something" generation. These entry-level employees have different work ethics than entry-level workers in the past. These young people see little need to start at the ground level and work their way up. Employers tell me twenty-something workers often resent doing tedious jobs. They expect to be hired immediately into management positions even though they may have few skills outside their formal education. They graduate from college fully expecting to land high-paying jobs just because they are college graduates, yet they may know little about job responsibilities.

It is vitally important for parents to teach children responsible work habits at an early age. Even young children can gain lifelong skills by accomplishing designated tasks.

> "Remember, your basic assignment as a parent is to work yourself out of a job."
>
> Paul Lewis

No More Bad Days

We try to help children verbalize their feelings by asking, "Are you having a bad day?" They quickly learn that the most effective response is to let you know how bad their day is going. Why should we encourage children to dwell on the negative aspects of their day? Recently I saw a family at the airport that was returning from Disneyworld. The eight year old of the family looked like a walking advertisement for Disney. She sported Mickey Mouse ears, a Minnie Mouse dress, Pluto socks, and a giant Lion King stuffed animal.

"Mom," she whined, "I'm having a horrible day." Her concerned mother wanted to know the details. "I lost the bow on my Lion King," the child explained.

Let's face reality! A lost bow doesn't constitute "a bad day." It might be a bad five-minute segment out of a totally fantastic day at Disneyworld. Let's help our children concentrate on the positive aspects of their lives.

Charles Stanley, author of *How to Keep Your Kids on Your Team* (Thomas Nelson), stresses the importance of teaching your child to have a positive outlook. Parents can explain the difference between failing and being a failure. Pessimistic children grow up to be pessimistic adults. So break the cycle by helping children see the positive side of life. To do that, we, first of all, have to have a positive attitude about life ourselves. Doesn't the Bible tell us: "in everything give thanks; for this is God's will for you in Christ Jesus" (1 Thes 5:18).

- Put things in perspective. "And we know that God causes all things to work together for good to those who love God, to those who are called according to His purpose" (Rom 8:28). Yes, it's painful to be cut from the basketball team, but it's not the end of life. Help your child make a list of all his or her past successes.

- Help him or her to evaluate if the current situation is short-term or long-term. Getting braces is traumatic, but it's a short-term situation providing long-term results.

- Share with your children experiences you have had where you needed to make a conscious effort to have an optimistic outlook.

- Make concrete plans to turn the negative situation into a positive one. Didn't get a part in the school play? Take acting lessons. Practice projecting your voice. Read a book on audition techniques. In other words, take action instead of complaining.

- Set an example by being optimistic. How often do you come home from work, moaning and groaning about your horrible day? "Whatever is true, whatever is honorable, whatever is right, whatever is pure, whatever is lovely, whatever is of good repute, if there is any excellence and if anything worthy of praise, let your mind dwell on these things" (Phil 4:8).

In our family, we've decided to avoid the phrase "I'm having a bad day" completely. Instead, we try to put the situation in perspective by saying something like, "I was irritated for a while during the traffic jam, but it was better when I listened to my new tape in the car."

> *Mama Said There'd Be Days Like This (But She Never Said Just How Many)* by Charlene Ann Braumbich, Servant Publications.
>
> *Stick a Geranium in Your Hat and Be Happy* by Barbara Johnson, Word Publishing.

Safety First

It's a whole lot more fun to hold theme parties and make creative projects than to discuss safety rules with your children. However, statistics tell us unintentional injuries are the number one cause of death in children and youth between the ages of one and twenty-four. Safety instruction is vital!

Here's an idea that might help to make it not quite so tedious. Rather than gathering the family and giving them a set of Red Cross rules and regulations, get everyone involved in a creative learning process. Use family members' talents to help them learn.

One family taught their dog to "Stop, Drop, and Roll," which is the basic life-saving technique if you are on fire. The trick became so popular the dog became a regular guest on the kindergarten class circuit. If you don't have a dog, or if your dog can't learn to scratch fleas on his own, or if you're just not in the mood to train your dog to stop, drop, and roll, maybe these ideas will appeal to you:

- Use teachable moments by asking your preschooler to tell you two safety rules about crossing the church parking lot as you walk together across the parking lot pavement.

- Establish an unusual but easily identifiable code word for the family. Instruct the children never to go with anyone who doesn't know the family's code word.

I heard a funny story about this. A father, getting off early from work, decided to pick up his first-grader after school. The surprised little girl refused to go with her father because he had forgotten the family code word. It took a phone call to Mom to convince the little girl it was OK to go with Dad. You can bet he never forgot the code word again!

Ideas for Keeping Your Family Safe

- Remove all loose drawstrings around sweatshirts that could get caught in bus doors or on playground equipment. Many major clothing manufacturers now use velcro or other fasteners. Ask family members to go through their closets to check for clothing with drawstrings.

- Some Red Cross departments offer family first-aid classes. Check to see if your local branch offers a class you could attend with your older children.

- The US Consumer Product Safety Commission states that an average of one child each month dies from strangulation by cords or chains on window coverings. Check your window covering cords so they are not tied together or hanging near a young child's crib or bed.

- Diagram an escape route on paper and then practice it together. Each child should "escape" from his or her room following the plan. Then everyone should meet at the safe meeting place (such as a mailbox or neighbor's house) established beforehand.
- Insist everyone in the family wear a seat belt in the car and helmets while riding bikes.

For additional safety and health tips, try the American Academy of Pediatrics on the Internet at www.aap.org.

> For a free checklist of home safety considerations, call 1-800-SAFE-HOME or send a SASE to: NSC PR Dept., 1121 Spring Lake Dr., Itasca, IL 60143.
>
> *On the Safe Side: Teach Your Child to Be Safe, Strong and Streetsmart* by Paula Stratman, Harper Perennial.

Enjoying Diversity

The trend today is for schools, youth groups, and businesses to encourage diversity. While many of us grew up in Leave-it-to-Beaver neighborhoods of all-one-race children, children now go to school with a wide variety of ethnic groups as well as children with special needs. Sometimes it comes as a surprise to young children when they find themselves in a reading group with children of another race or when they sit next to a child with a physical disability.

Jesus set a powerful example when he associated with powerful leaders and salt-of-the-earth fishermen. He cared about people regardless of their looks, income level, social standing, or race.

You can help your family celebrate diversity in these ways:

- Occasionally attend a church that has a worship style different from your regular church.
- Watch the local paper for notices about authors of various ethnic backgrounds who may be speaking in your area. Sit in on their presentations.
- Attend concerts given by international university students studying in your area.
- Write letters and draw pictures to a missionary family as a family project. Ask them for details about the foods, customs, and living conditions they are experiencing.
- Check out videos of foreign cultures and ethnic cookbooks from the library.
- Watch a video on China while eating homemade fortune cookies.
- Make apple strudel and view *The Sound of Music,* which was filmed in Austria.
- If friends celebrate Hanukkah or Kwanzaa, ask about their traditions. They may invite you to join them in their celebrations.
- Consider sponsoring a foreign exchange student. Rotary groups and foreign language classes look for families willing to open their home to an international student. If you are chosen to host a student, you'll experience a different culture firsthand by sharing customs, food, and language right in your own home.

The Kids' Multicultural Cook Book by Deanna Cook, Williamson Publishing.

The Multicultural Cookbook for Students by Carole Lisa Albyn and Lois Sinaiko Webb, Onyx Press.

Those Terrific Preschoolers

Watch a group of three to five year olds in the playground. They run, swing, sing, and imagine. Everything is new and exciting. They marvel at the intricacies of mixing dirt, wood, and water. They soon learn it is even more fun to run through the mud they make. Parents often find children of this age require a tremendous amount of supervision which requires an equal amount of energy. To truly enjoy your preschooler:

- Reward positive behavior. We often comment on preschoolers' misbehavior and ignore when they do what's expected of them. For continued positive results, thank them for coming down from the monkey bars when you call; acknowledge their cooperation at getting into the car seat; and find as many ways as possible to commend them for good behavior.

- Let young children be young children. It's not necessary to enroll your preschooler in every computer or sports program available. Let them be children who have time to dream, explore, play, and enjoy helping you sweep the kitchen floor.

- Learn to talk less and listen more. Tape record yourself for a few hours. You'll be amazed at how often you spew one directive after another toward your children. Children quickly learn to tune you out, so save the long monologues for important conversations. Instead of saying, "It's time to get our coats on to go to preschool. I'll get my coat and you get yours. Then we'll get in the car and go to school.... Don't forget your lunch." Instead, say, "Coat on. Time for preschool."

- Select appropriate activities for the child's age group. Pre schoolers have short attention spans. Asking them to cut out intricate hearts for Aunt Mary's Valentine produces frustration. Read a few child development books to give you a clear idea what three to five year olds can do.

• Have fun! This is a wonderful age where children delight in just being with you. Get on the floor and play blocks with them. Laugh at their silly knock-knock jokes and proudly display their artwork.

Preschoolers are certainly "labor intensive," but the payoff is an obedient, happy, affectionate child who likes being with you. Enjoy it now because this phase of childhood ends all too soon.

> Try a session of "child-directed play." Simply get on the floor and play with your child for fifteen minutes—without giving any suggestions or directions. Can you do it?

Great All-Around Activity Books

Some people create activities and special events from their own original ideas. Then there are those of us who need ideas from other sources. The following are books and magazines guaranteed to provide hundreds of ideas for games, crafts, and activities:

• *My First Paint Book* by Dawn Sirett, London: Dorling Kindersley, 1994.

• *Pretend Soup and Other Real Recipes* by Mollie Katzen and Ann Henderson, Berkely: Tricycle Press, 1994.

- *365 TV Free Activities You Can Do With Your Child* by Steve and Ruth Bennett, Bob Adams, Inc.
- *Wee Sing Around the World* (audio tape), Price Stern Sloan.
- *The Kids' Summer Handbook* by Jane Drake, Ann Lowe, Ticknor and Fields Books for Young Readers.
- *Paper Action Toys* by E. Richard Churchill, Sterling Publishing Co.
- *Einstein's Science Parties: Easy Parties for Curious Kids* by Shar Levin and Allison Grafton, John Wiley and Sons, Publishers.
- *The Human Body: An Interactive Guide to Your Body* by Steve Parker, Dorling Kindersly.
- *A Family Music Sampler* (audio tape) by Sample This!
- *The Multimedia Home Companion for Parents and Kids* by Christine Olson, Warner Books.
- *The Christmas Alphabet* by Robert Sabuda, Orchard Books.
- *Bill Nye the Science Guy: Dinosaurs, Outer Space, and Human Body* (videos) by Walt Disney Home Videos.
- *Fun Things To Do With Your Kids* by Carl Dreizler and Phil Phillips, Galahad Books.
- *What Do You Do After You Turn Off The TV?* by Frances Moore Lappé, Ballantine.
- *Rain or Shine Activity Book* by Joanna Cole and Stephanie Calmenson, William Morrow.

Additional Resources

- Purchase a copy of *Free Stuff for Kids* from Meadowbrook Press (18318 Minnetonka Blvd., Deephaven, MN 55391). The next time children are cooped inside, get out the book and send away for hundreds of free or low-cost items. It usually takes a postcard to order a variety of stickers, pencils, and posters.

- Order *Toll Free Numbers for Health Information*, published by the U.S. Department of Health and Human Services for $1.00. This booklet is a great resource for information on dozens of health care topics. National Health Information Center, Box 1133 Washington, DC, 20013-1133.

- Looking to give someone an unusual gift? For $36.00 you can name a star after your special person. The Star Directory provides a registration certificate and a location map. 1-800-500-3128.

- *The Art of Learning Catalog* offers unusual art supplies. Think what your child could do with holograph paper, wood mosaic squares, silly springs, shredded felt, and really big stencils. 1-800-627-2829.

- If you or your friends want up-to-date travel information, subscribe to *Have Children Will Travel.* This newsletter costs $39.00 and provides current and unusual family travel information. P.O. Box 152, Lake Oswego, OR 97034, (503) 699-5869.

- Encourage your child to enter the "Design a Dream Doll Contest." The winner receives a doll manufactured in the likeness of his or her sketch plus a trip to New York. Order the entry form by calling 1-800-567-8222.

- To help children choose appropriate role models, check into a set of videos called *Adventures From the Book of Virtues.* These thirty-minute videos use modern-day children to teach about characters such as Daniel and the Lions and Harriet Tubman and the Underground Railroad (Porchlight Entertainment Videos).

- *Beyond TV* is a quarterly publication for parents and teachers designed to be a resource for managing television use. $10.00 for four issues from: The Television Project, 11160 Veirs Mill Rd., L-15 Suite 277, Wheaton, MD 20902.

- The National Institute on Media and the Family offers a short checklist to help you evaluate your family's media habits. 1-888-672-5437.

Keep Those Catalogs Coming!

Instead of running from store to store looking for gifts or craft items, put up your feet and try mail-order catalog shopping.

- *Flaghouse Physical Education Catalog* offers regulation foam bowling balls specially weighted for easy grip—ideal for those times when you set up a bowling alley in your hall. You could get sets of *No Point Darts,* hundreds of various sized balls, magical activity boxes, and even a *Ka-Boing Ball.* (You'll have to order the catalog to see what that is: 1-800-793-7900.)

- For additional sports and movement supplies, *Sportime* catalog offers eight-inch-long space shooters, juggling supplies, peacock feathers, and assorted sized hula hoops. Catalog available from 1-800-283-5700.

- If your children enjoy arts and crafts, *S & S Catalog* will keep them occupied for hours. Inexpensive craft items are offered individually or in complete kits. (Great for birthday parties, scout groups, and Sunday school classes.) You'll find everything from pre-cut wooden bird house kits to tile trivets to a seashell jewelry-making pack: 1-800-243-9232.

- The *Re-Print Corporation* offers a catalog of discounted school and craft supplies. Here's where you can order colorful feathers, plastic "wiggle" eyes, sequins, colored pasta, and all sizes of paint brushes: 1-800-248-9171.

- For a free catalog of cake and cookie decorating supplies, contact Sweet Celebrations, 7009 Washington Ave. S., Edina, MN 55439, 1-800-480-2505.

- Do you have games with crucial missing pieces? Instead of buying a whole new game, simply order the parts you need. To order replacement parts for Milton Bradley games, call 212-645-2403. Write Parker Brothers Games for their replacement parts at Box 1012, Beverly, MA 01915.

The wide variety of unusual games and art supplies available from these catalogs provides the opportunity for imaginative play. Next birthday, instead of a traditional gift, set a monetary limit, and let the child choose something from one of these catalogs. For Christmas, ask children to circle items they want. When relatives ask what to buy, give them the list and let them order in their price range.

Encouraging
Creativity
While
Outdoors

The Great Outdoors

Children naturally gravitate to outdoor play. Outside they can yell, run without fear of knocking over a vase, and feel the freedom of open spaces. Those few times when children need some ideas to fill their time, it just takes a suggestion to inspire more creative play on their own. Try some of these ideas:

- Have a bike race with a twist. Racers start at the finish line and attempt to reach the start line...last. The slowest rider wins! Participants must ride as slowly as possible without putting a foot on the ground.

- Have you ever seen figure skaters trace intricate figure eights on the ice? Set up your own bicycle course by drawing a figure eight chalk line on a smooth surface. Or draw wavy lines. The object is to "trace" the chalk line while riding your bike.

- Set up a sprinkler and try jumping rope next to the spurting water.

- Gather the neighborhood children for a game of group hide-and-seek or "sardines." As usual, one person is "it" and only that person *hides*. All the other children cover their eyes until the designated count is complete. Everyone races to find the person who is hiding. When someone finds the one who's hiding, he or she hides with the "hider." They all scrunch together until the whole group is hidden and only one person is looking.

- If you have a large, sturdy ball, challenge children to see how long they can lay on it with only their stomach touching the ball.
- Play an old-fashioned game of pickle. One player stands between two other children. They throw the ball to each other without the center person catching the ball.
- Feeling brave? Set out nontoxic finger paints and let children decorate your garage door or a side of the house. Don't worry—it easily washes off with a hose.

A Tribute To Buster

According to an article in *Recreation Canada*, the main outdoor recreational activity in the year 2001 will be bird watching. Be a trendsetter and get a headstart on this family activity. Just think, no matter where you live, the chances are high you'll spot birds without leaving home. It might be a simple crow or a robin, but watching—really watching—a bird soar through the sky is still an amazing sight.

Several years ago I gave my husband a thirty-dollar Koi for his fish pond. We named our expensive goldfish Buster and watched him swim along with the other fish among the lily pads. Buster had been enjoying his new home for less than twenty-four hours when we looked out the window just in time to see a giant heron take one quick poke in the water and spear Buster! The bird looked magnificent as it soared over the trees, but I felt very sorry for the helpless Buster. Hopefully the birds you watch will provide enjoyment without the pain of seeing them carry off a thirty-dollar fish.

- Bird watching requires no equipment, although binoculars definitely add to the enjoyment by giving a close-up view. Our friends kept their binoculars on the windowsill to observe close-up construction of a swallow's nest on their porch.

- Attract birds to your area by providing a variety of feeders and types of seed. It might take a few days, but soon your outdoor bird restaurant will be very busy.

- Purchase a bird identification book and keep track of the birds you sight. Younger children can draw pictures of the birds they see.

Summer Bird Feeding by John V. Davis, Prism Creative Group.

The Audubon Society offers a catalog of field guides and bird watching information. 1-212-979-3119.

Let It Snow, Let It Snow

Those of us lucky to live in an area where it snows know the excitement of running outside for the first snow of the year. School children rush to the windows, eager to get outside and build snowmen or catch the cold white flakes on their tongues.

To celebrate snow days:

- Begin with snowman pancakes. Make three silver-dollar-size pancakes so the edges touch to create a snowman. Use raisins for eyes and down the pancake snowman's tummy for buttons.

- Find fresh clean snow. Put 3 cups into a bowl. Add 2 tablespoons milk, 1/4 cup sugar, and 1 teaspoon vanilla and mix well. You've just made snow ice cream.

- Make a series of snow people guards to stand at the entrance of your driveway.
- Make a snowman or snow fort. Use a spray bottle to spray on a variety of colored water solutions for a multi-colored effect that will be the envy of the neighborhood.
- Challenge each other to find animal tracks in fresh snow. You might not find Bigfoot, but you'll probably see a few bird or deer tracks. If there are no animal prints, identify boot prints made by fellow family members.
- Make a family of snow angels.
- If sledding, experiment with a variety of riding possibilities. Try cardboard, plastic bags, and even giant mixing bowls. Be careful, though, as safety must be your first consideration. Only sled on open hillsides away from trees, rocks, and stumps.
- Make and freeze snowballs for a July snowball fight. (When July comes, be sure to let the snowballs thaw a bit before throwing them.)
- If you worry about children getting hurt during snowball fights, set up a few targets. Encourage them to throw snowballs into an empty trash can or use the basketball hoop as a target. One mother hung a large inner tube on the side of the house away from windows and watched children try to throw snowballs through the center of the tube.
- Make a heart-shaped outline in the snow. Fill in the design with birdseed, bread pieces, and fruit to make a special feast for the birds.
- End a day of snow activities with hot chocolate and a favorite book.

> We've all heard that no two snowflakes are alike. In the late 1800s a farmer photographed 5,000 snowflakes and found they were all different.

Beach Bonanza

Many of us have fond memories of lazy summer days at the beach. (We didn't even use sunscreen!) Miles of sand, driftwood, and the possibility of countless discoveries under rocks make the beach an ideal place for family activities.

Building sand castles and jumping over waves occupy children most of the day. But if you're looking for a few additional beach-related activities, try these ideas:

- Throughout the year collect a variety of plastic jugs and juice containers to use as sand forms. The shapes help add architectural interest to sand castles.

- Take along several jugs of water and a large bucket. Just before you get in the car to go home, have children stand in the bucket and rinse them off with the fresh water. A quick hop into the car results in less sand on their bodies and in your car.

- Play a giant game of tic-tac-toe in the sand. Use a shovel to smooth down the sand. Carefully dig the four-line grid. Then, take turns marking the "X" and "O" in the sand with a stick or shovel.

- Set up a miniature golf course by building sand castles and water holes. Dig holes and place buckets in the sand. Attempt a hole-in-one as you maneuver past mounds of shells. Bring plastic golf clubs along, or simply use a piece of driftwood and a ball.

- Collect driftwood and create your own village in the sand. Stick pieces in the sand and balance shells or starfish on top.
- Sand can be formed into more than sand castles. Using molds or empty buckets, try making a giant octopus or sea monster.
- Check to see if there is a local sand-sculpting contest scheduled for your area. You'll be amazed at the intricate designs.
- Time your visit to the seashore for sunset or sunrise. The results can be breathtaking.

Extras for the beach! Moist towelettes, long-sleeved shirts, trash bags for wet clothes and garbage, children's sunglasses or wide-brimmed hats, plenty of water to drink.

Old-Fashioned Block Party

Adults often lament how isolated neighborhoods have become. We might wave to someone mowing their lawn but seldom take time to chat or even to borrow the infamous cup of sugar like in "the good old days."

Let your family be the catalyst to bring neighbors together for fun and fellowship by organizing a block party. If you live on a quiet street or cul-de-sac, check with city officials about obtaining a permit to close the street to traffic. If that is not an option, use your backyard or combine with neighbors and use their front yard also.

After deciding on a basic format, let your children design the invitation. Be sure to tell people if they should bring their own dishes and eating utensils. One neighborhood started out small by asking everyone to bring a potluck dessert. The event was so successful it has now turned into a full-fledged four-hour extravaganza with music, food, and games. Distribute the invitations and follow up with phone calls if you think neighbors are hesitant to attend an unfamiliar event.

To add to the fun:

- Ask local firefighters or police officers to make a public relations visit. Children enjoy sitting on the firetruck or in a police car and scaring their parents by turning on the siren.
- Provide icebreaker activities for parents. Let children make silly name tags for adults, or conduct a tricycle race for grownups.
- Set up a few carnival-type booths for children and parents. You won't need prizes because just throwing beanbags and knocking down bowling pins as often as they want is enough reward for children.
- Ask a neighbor to bring an ice cream maker. Ask another to help haul away the excess trash after the get-together.
- Enjoy the smiles and waves of recognition you'll receive after new friendships are formed.

> Provide name tags for everyone at your gathering. It's embarrassing to admit you can't remember the name of someone who lives on your street.

Let's Go Fly a Kite

Nothing beats the feel of wind hitting your body as you attempt to get a kite into the air. It usually takes a few attempts to launch the kite, so tell children they'll need to be patient before you join Mary Poppins in singing, "Let's go fly a kite...."

- Find a suitable location away from power lines and trees. A flat surface will prevent the children from tripping as they run to get the kite aloft.
- If this is your child's first attempt at kite flying, use a manufactured kite to raise the level of success. Colorful kites made by preschoolers are cute but lack the strength and design needed to get up in the air.
- Remind children that kites need wind to fly. I've seen many a frustrated child attempt to launch a kite on a windless day. Ask your child to observe signs of wind, such as hair blowing in their face or leaves fluttering on tree branches.
- If your children are very young, have them hold the kite while you run to get it into the air. Be sure to tell your child it's OK to let go of the kite when there is tension on the twine!
- Try a variety of materials for the kite tail. Find out what happens when you use crepe paper, surveyor's tape, or cotton gauze.
- If it begins to rain, come inside. Electricity travels along a wet kite line.
- If your children want to make kites but lack skill in aerodynamic design, use them for decoration in their rooms.

Planting and Pruning

When God made the earth, he certainly used creativity in the variety of plants and flowers he gave us to enjoy. Look at the contrast in size, texture, and smell between a sunflower and a rose. If you have a yard, your children probably have a basic awareness of how things grow. Even if you live in a city apartment, there are many opportunities to foster a sense of wonder at how tiny seeds grow into magnificent flowers or towering trees.

Try some of these activities to increase your family's understanding of nature:

- Plant a vegetable garden, even if it means putting a few radish seeds in a tub on your balcony. If space permits, give your child a small plot of dirt to garden. After planting, weeding, and harvesting their crops, children might even *eat* the vegetables. Imagine that!

- Take a walk and observe the durability of weeds growing between rocks or in sidewalk cracks.

- Some families plant a tree in their yard when a child is born. They then measure the growth of both the tree and the child on the child's birthday.

- No room for a garden? Contact the local Master Gardeners or Parks and Recreation Department to see if they have community gardens. For a small fee, they'll assign you a tilled plot of land where you can grow flowers or vegetables.

- Grow narcissus or amaryllis bulbs in your house during the winter to bring springtime beauty into your home.

Join the National Arbor Day Foundation for only $10.00. You'll receive ten trees selected to grow in your area. 100 Arbor Ave., Nebraska City, NE 68410.

Nature All Around

Preschool and kindergarten teachers know the importance of using natural materials in teaching. You can provide your children with many creative experiences using natural materials. Here are a few ideas:

- Sand or water tables filled with mud, sand, or potting soil provide a wonderful sensory experience.

- If the weather is too severe to go outside, bring a bucket of dirt into your house. Let your children make stick people villages complete with lakes and streams in the dirt.

- Before you mow the dandelions in your yard, help your children make a flower crown. Form a crown from lightweight wire, and then use thread or dental floss to tie the flowers to it. Place the crown on the child's head, and they are king or queen of the forest.

- Look for four-leaf clovers.

- Stand a box on its side and put moss, twigs, and rocks inside for a nature craft diorama.

- Collect a large assortment of small twigs and branches you find lying on the ground. Decorate empty cardboard tubes. Then insert as many sticks as possible into the tube. These make great fire starters for people with wood stoves or fireplaces.

- If pine cones are abundant in your area, glue them onto a heavy piece of doughnut-shaped cardboard. Add a bow and you have a nice wreath.
- Decorate your mailbox for Christmas with a garland of evergreen branches.
- Collect pine cones to make cone creatures. Use pipe cleaners, wiggle eyes, and fabric scraps to turn ordinary pine cones into unusual woodland creatures.
- Play "he loves me, he loves me not" by pulling the petals off a daisy.
- Select an unusual-looking piece of wood, about six to eight inches long. String twigs, rocks, and pine cones from the main wood piece for a mobile.

Good Earth Art by Mary Ann Kohl, Bright Ring Publishing.
Nature Crafts by Imogene Forte, Incentive Publications.
Even New York City offers nature walks in city parks. Call 718-383-6363 for details.

Wet and Wild

Families and youth groups can rent community swimming pools for fun and exercise. If you have the pool entirely to yourselves, plan a few water-related activities in addition to free swim time. Here are some pool activities:

- Relay races take on new meaning when played in the water. Have teams walk back and forth across the pool. Have volunteers hold hula hoops for people to crawl through. Do a race with participants blowing soap bubbles as they race toward the finish line.

- Plan a spontaneous synchronized swimming exhibition. Select five or six of your most outgoing participants to stand waist-deep in the water. Designate a leader, turn on the music, and watch the fun. The results are hilarious as everyone tries to follow the leader's moves while smiling and looking confident—although they have no idea when to turn or spin through the water!

- In addition to a big-splash contest, award prizes for the small-splash contest. Have a group of serious-looking judges using scorecards judge the events.

- Float plastic ducks in the pool as participants stand around the edge. Throw plastic rings around the ducks' necks to earn points for your team.

- Place two teams facing each other about ten feet apart. Hold a string or plastic cord just under the water, an equal distance from each team. Throw a table tennis ball in front of each team. Their goal is to make waves and try to get their ball across the line into the other team's territory.

- Walk-the-plank is fun for participants. Select an adult to walk off the diving board as children eight and under throw wet sponges at the person "walking the plank."

Star Light, Star Bright

Taking a walk in the evening or camping under the stars is a variation from everyday routines. One family had a tradition of celebrating every full moon with outdoor snacks and stories. If it rained or was cloudy, they hung a gold beach ball in the living room and celebrated anyway.

Here are some additional activities to try after sunset:

- Purchase a star chart to help identify constellations. For a special treat, go to an area away from street and house lights so that you can see the stars more clearly.

- If there are fireflies in your area, catch them in a clear plastic container. Time the intervals between flashes. Then release them.

- Call a local astronomy club or university to see if they'd let you look at stars through one of their high-powered telescopes.

- When there is a meteor shower, make a point to stay up and see it. The wonder of "shooting stars" streaking across the skies makes up for any lost sleep.

- Most of us recognize the Big Dipper but have difficulty identifying any other constellation. Name your own! Check out the stars and you may find "Dad's mustache" or "Jordan's soccer ball."

- Stay up past bedtime, go outside in your pajamas, and enjoy watching the stars. Serve croissants (which look like a quarter moon). Be sure to bring insect repellent.

- Several children's magazines deal with astronomy and the great outdoors. *Your Big Backyard* is geared toward preschoolers, while *Ranger Rick* appeals to six to twelve year olds. Contact *National Wildlife Foundation*, 1400 16th St. NW, Washington, DC 20036-2266, 1-800-432-6564. *Chickadee*, a magazine for children under nine, offers ten issues per year, filled with experiments and stunning photographs. *Young Naturalist Foundation*, 225 Great Arrow Ave., Buffalo, NY 14207-3082, 1-416-946-0606.

Rocks and Twigs

Even if you live in the downtown area of a city, there are opportunities to expose your children to the wonders of nature. I remember working as a counselor at Forest Home Christian Conference Center many years ago. One particular week, a group of children from the inner city of Los Angeles arrived for a week of fun in the great outdoors. Those children were amazed at the variety of trees, flowers, and rocks all around us—trees, flowers, and rocks we all took for granted. One nine year old, looking at the San Bernardino mountains, asked, "How long did it take you to paint that picture?" I explained she was seeing an actual mountain and she replied, "I thought you painted a giant picture of a mountain so we would have an idea what a mountain looked like."

Observing birds build a nest, collecting driftwood on a stormy day at the beach, or making a centerpiece out of pine cones costs nothing. The opportunities to appreciate God's outdoor world are endless. Try some of these:

- Go on a "rock walk." Hike around the neighborhood or in a nearby park. See who can find the shiniest rock or the rock with the most unusual shape. Display the rocks on a window sill when you get home.
- Make a nature collage from small twigs, pebbles, and leaves. Family members can make individual collages or work together on one large group project.
- Remember the wax paper prints we made in elementary school? Simply place a sheet of wax paper on top of light cardboard. Arrange a design of leaves on the wax paper. Cover with another piece of wax paper and one sheet of construction paper. Have an

adult use a warm iron to seal the leaf picture inside.

- Pick a variety of flowers and place between absorbent paper or paper towels. Lay them on a table and place several heavy books on top. In a few weeks the flowers are flat and dried, making them ready for a variety of arts and crafts projects.

- Start a collection of nature items. How about: feathers, pine cones, moss, tree bark, shells, sand dollars, seeds, or unique twigs?

> *God's Quiet Things* by Nancy Sweetland (Eerdmans Publishing) describes the wonders of nature when we're quiet enough to really listen.

Cool Fun

It's hot, you're stuck at home, and everyone is cranky. When the kids beg you to install a swimming pool, and you're not about to do that, try some of these ideas to cool off and chill out:

- Get the kids into their swimsuits. Throw apples into a small wading pool and have them bob for apples.

- Set up the sprinkler and join your children in cooling off by running through the spraying water with them.

- Wash the car and don't worry if a water fight starts.

- Give young children clean paint brushes and buckets of clear water to "paint" the house.

- Play "Sponge Splat." Soak several sponges in cold water. Have a volunteer stand against the side of the house. Take turns throwing the sponge close to the "victim," trying to make him or her flinch. (Head and face area is off limits.)

- Wet sponges are useful for playing "water, water, sponge." Everyone sits in a circle. The person who is *it* walks around the outside, tapping people on the head saying, "water, water, water...." At one point, *it* plops a wet sponge on a person's head. That person jumps up and tries to catch him or her.

- Lay on the grass with an ice cube on your stomach. See how long you can last before it gets too cold or you get the giggles.

- If you normally have bath crayons in the tub, bring them outside and let children use them to decorate the wading pool or large buckets of water.

Your family can actually enjoy the heat with these cooling activities. One mother living in Palm Springs went so far as to plan Christmas in July to get her family thinking about a cooler time. They made a paper tree, exchanged white elephant gifts, and sang Christmas carols around the air conditioner.

The Roving Playground

Ever had one of those glorious days without an urgency of demands to meet? When it happens to you next time, use that day to schedule a playground and park day:

- Get a local map and mark out the parks and school playgrounds within a reasonable driving distance.

- Then rank those parks on a scale of one to ten with one being everyone's favorite location.

- Pack a lunch for all of you, a good book for yourself, toys for the kids, and you're off.

- *Leave* a park only when there is a unanimous decision that it's time to move to the next location.

A dad with three children, ages ranging from five to twelve, found this a perfect way to spend a Saturday. "The kids loved going to a park, playing for an hour, then driving to another park, swimming two hours there if the mood hit us, and so on. Visiting various school playgrounds added to the variety. If there was a store close by, everyone would walk over, get a treat, and then go back to the park."

Another parent adapted the idea for days when the whole family participated in a thorough house cleaning. "We'd all work hard until noon, then go to a fast food restaurant for lunch. Afterwards, we'd visit one park after another. The highlight was bringing out the flashlights at night and playing by the glow of flashlights in a deserted park."

When families complain about the high cost of entertainment, it's possible they are overlooking free resources. Even the smallest communities have a school playground and a local park. Part of the enjoyment for children is the luxury of time to play. Imagine how you would have felt as a child if your parents said, "You can play at the park as long as you want." A mother of three preschoolers confessed, "A playground day is a treat for me. While the kids play, I write letters, pay bills, and organize photos. When they get bored, we move to another park, and I have another hour to read my magazine."

"A happy family is but an earlier heaven."

John Bowring

Creative

Travel

Tips

Travel Tips

Sooner or later, you'll find yourself at the airport preparing to spend several hours in a cramped plane with your children. Instead of dreading the time, look at it as an ideal way to teach children travel skills while having an adventure. If your children are at least eight to nine years old, give them complete control as you enter the airport. Let them:

- find the correct ticket counter,
- check in, and
- locate the boarding gate.

Our seven year old travels with me frequently and for the past three years has been responsible for finding our boarding area. (We allow extra time because we may end up at B-6 instead of B-26!)

A family with two elementary-aged children always let them sit together several rows away from the parents. The children were on their best behavior because they felt grownup and independent sitting by themselves. It gave their parents a nice break also!

This same family let their children fill out the paperwork and speak with airline representatives when their luggage ended up on another flight. It is easy for parents to step in and take control, but when we do so, we deprive our children of becoming confident in dealing with issues that come up while traveling. Look at the entire travel process as a chance to be together and a chance to learn. Is your flight delayed? It's not so bad. You're not standing on a snowy runway, hungry and cold, are you? Probably not. More than likely you are inside an airport that's heated or air-conditioned. There are places to sit and restrooms available. So relax and enjoy your family. Play games, walk from one end of the airport to the other, people-watch, or go to the airport chapel and have family devotions.

> "Family Travel Times" is an informative newsletter with worldwide travel news for families. 212-477-5524.

Vacations = Memories

"The fondest memories people have of their pasts tend to involve family outings and vacations," states Professor Mihaly Csikszentmihalyi in his book *Benefits of Leisure*, Venture Publishing. So get packed (even if it is just for a two-day trip) and get ready for fun. Here are some ways to create fond memories:

Don't worry about paying for a hotel or finding a restaurant. Instead, change houses with a friend for the weekend. Your children will enjoy playing with "new" toys, and you will get to relax in someone else's easy chair. Just being in a different neighborhood makes going to the store or taking a walk a novel experience.

Try a new experience on vacation. If you've never gone clam-digging or visited an art museum, this is the time to try. We often keep within our comfort zones and avoid anything that produces anxiety. Since you're more relaxed on vacation, it's easier to feel adventurous and eat that first bite of ostrich meat.

If a hotel stay is in your plan, call the hotel's 800 number and ask about special discounts. Many hotels offer free children's meals or family rates. A few toll-free numbers are:

- Comfort Inn 800-221-2222
- Days Inn 800-325-2525
- Hilton 800-445-8667
- Hyatt 800-233-1234
- Sheraton 800-325-3535

If you live in the city, drive to the country and stop at a U-pick berry field or just walk alongside a fence and experience what cows *really* smell like!

Give each child an equal-sized backpack or tote bag. It's up to them to pack their favorite games and books. Just watch out for crayons if they'll be in a hot car.

For a free list of 375 convention and visitors bureaus, send a SASE to: International Association of Convention Visitors Bureaus, Box 758, Champaign, IL 61824.

Go to the Head of the Class

Looking for a slightly different family vacation this year? Something affordable? A place that holds your interest as well as that of younger family members? Discover the wide variety of college campuses that offer all-inclusive vacation packages. Your family will be lodged in clean, durable, and not very fancy dormitories. Children love eating in the school's cafeteria, swimming in the campus pools, and playing in the college sports facilities.

There are a few established programs, and they include:

- Family Vacation Center at the Santa Barbara campus of the University of California (UC), where parents can enjoy lectures by UC staff, tennis, golf, and aerobics. Children can play in age-appropriate groups. In the evening the whole family can gather for talent shows, games, and songs. Phone 805-893-3123.

- The Chautauqua Institution in Chautauqua, New York, invites "students" of all ages to expand their creative interests. Daily classes offer drama, crafts, writing, and music along with various sports. Evenings are reserved for storytelling, puppet shows, and concerts. Phone: 800-836-ARTS.

- The National Wildlife Federation sponsors conservation-related summits in selected states. Adults attend field trips and classes, while children enjoy age-appropriate activities. As with most of these programs, families participate in evening programs together. Phone 800-245-5484.

- Once again Disney develops a successful idea. The Disney Institute in Orlando offers the chance to learn film-making, computer animation, or acting. Many classes are taught by high-profile experts in their field. Lodging, classes, and evening entertainment come with the complete family package. Phone 800-496-6337.

Not everyone finds these pre-packaged vacations to their liking. They do, however, offer a convenient and low-stress way to spend time together without paying exorbitant daily hotel rates and living through restaurant hassles.

Great American Learning Vacations, Fodor's Travel Publications. *50 Great Family Vacations,* Globe Pequot Press. *Super Family Vacations* by Martha Shirk and Nancy Kiepper, Harper Books.

Ice Cream for Breakfast

If you are a typical family, you envision vacations on the French Riviera, but end up visiting Aunt Matilda in Indiana where you go to the state fair. Don't grieve—family vacations can be fun as well as being inexpensive. An article in *Visions* magazine (R. Couchman, Feb. 1988, pg. 4) stated that leisure is the single most important force in developing cohesive, healthy relationships between husbands and wives, parents and children. The simple process of being together without strict time schedules and planned activities renews family bonds.

A key factor in vacation planning is to make sure it provides a change from everyday routines. One woman fondly recalls her most vivid vacation memory. Her dad and sister had gone bowling, so she and her mother went to a movie. As they left the theater, she sighed and said, "Mom, I'd just love to see that movie again." Without missing a beat, her mother turned around and said, "Why not? We're on vacation. Let's go back in." Forty years later, she still remembers that moment of spontaneous fun.

In many families, Dad always drives the car while Mom referees the squabbling in the back seat. "My greatest joy on vacations is that I drive while my husband does the entertaining," one woman told me. "He actually enjoys playing the Alphabet License game, and I enjoy driving without having to deal with the kids." The arrangement works for them.

So you're on vacation and your son wants to eat ice cream for breakfast? Go ahead and let him. He'll remember the experience more than he would the purchase of a cheap trinket in a gift shop. If you can't make it to the French Riviera this year, make the most of your vacation by providing inexpensive and spontaneous fun:

- Some families find it easier to give each child a set amount of spending money at the beginning of vacation than to dole it out all through the vacation. If the child chooses to spend it all on the first day, he or she must live with the consequences.

- Make sure each person gets an equal say in the day's activities. For some three year olds, the highlight of each day is using the ice machine in the hotel hallway.

- Get a local paper and find out about farmer's markets or community festivals.

> Entertainment Publications publishes discount coupon booklets for over 125 US and Canadian locations. Purchasing one for your vacation destination could save you money on hotels and food. 800-477-3234.

Back Seat Antics

Whether it's a sixteen-hour trip to Grandma's or a ten-minute drive to school, there's something about being confined in a car that brings out the worst in children.

Who can concentrate on driving with "Mom, Jason's breathing my air!" coming from the back seat? Instead of having everyone arrive at your destination in a grumpy mood, try a little creativity (and planning ahead) to solve many of the irritations:

- Begin by putting the responsibility on your children. Ask them, "What can we do to reduce bickering in the car?" They might suggest a car calendar to document who rides in the front seat, so everyone has a fair chance. One brother and sister suggested they eat their breakfast in the car on the fifteen-minute drive to school. The parents agreed as long as the mess was minimal. Now the once-raucous ride is calm as the children eat bagels and fruit, and sip juice from spill-proof mugs while Christian music plays. Other ideas to avoid back seat hassles include:

- On long trips, pass around a bag filled with odds and ends such as ribbons, a dirty sock, hair brush, or plastic cup. Have children take turns reaching into the bag, selecting an item, and then using it in an unconventional way. For example, the dirty sock could be used as a unique way to put hair into a pony tail. The plastic cup transforms to a microphone and an impromptu version of Karaoke.

- Keep a book of jokes and riddles in the car. Designate a child to be the "on-road comedian."

- Have informal devotions. (Just make sure the driver doesn't close his or her eyes to pray.) Let a child read a Bible verse while another child picks a favorite song to sing.

- Look at the license plate of a nearby car. Make up acronyms from the letters on the license plates. For example, CSP could stand for "Chocolate Solves Problems." DLW might be "Dad Loves Watermelon."

> Travel Activity Books: *Travel Games for the Family* by Marie Boatress, Canyon Creek Press; *"Are We There Yet?" Travel Games for Kids* by Richard Salter, Prince Paperbacks.

Museum Exploration

"**N**o, Mom! Not a trip to a boring art museum." Since most children gravitate only to hands-on children's museums, plan a few ways to make "adult museums" interesting.

If you're fortunate enough to live close to the Smithsonian Museum, the New York City Museum of Art, or another large museum, take advantage of staff-led programs and tours. For those of us who don't live near such museums, we'll just have to use creativity to show our children a variety of art styles found in small, local museums.

If going to a museum is new for your children, keep the experience short. Walk through two or three exhibits, visit the gift shop, check out the water fountain, and head back home.

For a more in-depth experience:

- Purchase a few postcards in the gift shop *before* your tour. Have the children look for the actual exhibits or paintings depicted on the postcards.

- If possible, visit the museum ahead of time alone. Make a list of distinctive items found throughout the museum. When you return with your children, give them the list. Soon they'll happily be searching for a painting of a woman wearing one red shoe or for a mobile made from paper clips.

- If children show particular interest in a painting, ask them to study it carefully and stand in the same position as the model in the painting. If there are several subjects in the painting, children can "freeze" in a diorama position in front of it.
- Make sure children are well-fed and rested before the excursion. Don't feel you have to see everything in the museum in one visit.

Your children may not become art fanatics, but they will be exposed to a variety of artistic styles. More than likely, the next painting or sculpture they make will reveal new ideas gained from the museum experience.

> A series of art appreciation books covering many artists is called *"What Makes a Picasso a Picasso?"* or *"What Makes a Van Gogh a Van Gogh?"* (Viking Books).

Modern-Day Hostels

Looking for low cost accommodations while traveling with your family? Try staying in a youth hostel. Many of us envision hostels only for teenage backpackers hitchhiking across the country, but the majority of hostels today gear their accommodations for all ages and often welcome families.

On our last trip to Europe, we spent the first night in a charming pension filled with antiques and delicate knickknacks. We also spent that first night telling our four-year-old daughter, "Don't touch that. It's fragile. Be quiet, people are sleeping!" The next night found us in a clean, comfortable family room in a youth hostel. It included four twin beds, table, sink, and small bathroom. Best of all, Sondra could move around the room without fear of breaking something. In addition, breakfast was included in the nominal fee. She eagerly joined a group of German schoolchildren going through the breakfast line. No one told her to be quiet.

Some hostels require you to complete a small chore before leaving. I still treasure the picture of my husband wearing a frilly apron as the hostel housemother explained how to run the dishwasher. My job consisted of wiping down two tables—much easier than my at-home chores!

A sampling of youth hostels:

- Stay in an actual teepee on Vashon Island, Washington.
- Banana Bungalow Hostels offer shuttle service between southern California tourist attractions. In Hollywood, the 250-bed hostel offers a pool, restaurant, theater, and parking.
- There's even a Big Apple Hostel in New York City for inexpensive lodging.
- A German youth hostel is located in a magnificent castle overlooking the Rhine river.

Hostelling International, 733 15th St. NW #840, Washington, DC 20005. (202) 783-6161. Provides a listing of five thousand hostels in seventy countries, plus membership information. Also available on the Internet at www.hostels.com/hostel.welcome.html.

Saving Souvenirs

Y ou've just completed a long-anticipated trip to the Grand Canyon. Maybe your family spent the three-day weekend visiting a historical site. After washing all the dirty laundry from the trip, you're faced with a pile of memorabilia ranging from brochures to postcards, plastic thimbles to rocks and sticks. What can you do to display and store souvenirs?

- One mother made lightweight flannel blankets for each of her children when they were toddlers. The travel blankets had their names appliquéd on them. On a trip, she purchased and sewed on the blanket souvenir patches of zoos, tourist attractions, and the state itself. This provided an easy way to remember past trips, and it also served as a comfort item when away from home.

- Have children purchase postcards on a daily basis and jot down their thoughts and feelings. Mail the postcards to themselves at home. When you arrive home, children will enjoy receiving the postcards they sent.

- Sew several plastic lock-top bags together at the bottom. Give children this "book" to store ticket stubs or whatever else they want to save as a reminder of their trip.

- Purchase a blank, fabric-covered book for each child. Keep scissors, glue, and a stapler in the car to add flat souvenirs to their travel journal.

- To avoid arguments about bringing home six-foot pieces of driftwood or other large objects, give each child a clear plastic box with a snap-on lid. All souvenirs obtained on the trip must fit inside the child's box.

- Create a table top display showing souvenirs the whole family obtained on the trip.

For a list of family travel resources, send $1.00 to:
Family Travel Catalog, Carousel Press,
P.O. Box 6038, Albany, CA 94706-0038.

Hometown Tours

Many children think the world consists of their home, school, and the closest McDonald's. A simple way to expand your children's awareness of other people and what they do is to arrange personalized tours of local factories and businesses. It's easier than you think. Simply call a place you'd like to visit and explain you are trying to help your children learn more about the community where they live. Besides the usual tours of fire or police stations, consider some of these options:

- A local radio station agreed to give a tour to a family whose ten-year-old son wanted to be a disc jockey. After seeing the variety of equipment and personnel, the ecstatic boy got invited to say on-the-air, "And now it's time for the weather report."
- Your children's school becomes a very different place in summer. A mother arranged for her two children to visit their "deserted" school in July. It surprised them to see how many people like custodians and secretaries worked to improve the school throughout the summer. A highlight of the tour included a peek into the hallowed teacher's lounge!
- Check local zoos and aquariums to see if they offer behind-the-scenes tours. Some zoos offer an opportunity to participate in a

"zoo snooze," when participants pay to spend the night at the zoo.

- One bakery offered to provide a tour as long as the family agreed to arrive at 5:00 A.M. on a Saturday morning to watch the baking process. The children were given a bag of warm doughnuts and gained an appreciation for people who work while others sleep. Now, whenever they drive by a bakery, someone says, "Remember how we helped pour flour into those huge mixing bowls? And remember how the baker gets up at 3:00 A.M. to get the bread baked in time? I never knew people had to go to work so early!"

> *Playing Smart: A Parents Guide to Enriching Offbeat Learning Activities for Ages 4-14* by Susan K. Perry, Free Spirit Publishing.

More Family Field Trips

Larger organizations often provide structured tours for schools or scout groups. Smaller businesses or community services rarely receive requests for tours. So when you call them, they are usually delighted to have you visit. Is there a local artist in your community? How about visiting a company that manufactures cat box filler?

The library may not seem a very thrilling place to visit, yet one family greatly enjoyed a behind-the-scenes tour. They stared in amazement as employees repaired the books. Everyone vowed to take better care of their library books after seeing the coffee stains, ripped pages, and other damage!

A quick look through the Yellow Pages provides a wealth of possible family field trip information. Pick up the phone and call:

- The Humane Society—take a dog for a walk when you're there.
- A grocery store—kids love the giant walk-in coolers and the free samples if the store has a bakery.
- A dance studio.
- A local dairy—you might get to milk a cow.
- A courtroom—schedule to watch a case in court.
- A physical fitness center.
- Florist shops or a nursery.
- A recycling center. Take cans or scrap metal to a recycling center and ask for a behind-the-scenes tour.
- Even a manufacturing plant offers opportunities to see giant machines and assembly line operations.

Don't forget behind-the-scenes tours of local bowling alleys, skating rinks, swimming pools, and the post office.

> Remember to send a thank-you note to the people leading your tour. Have children include drawings or personal postscripts.

Creative
Culinary
Experiences

Mealtime Magic

Sometimes the hardest task of the day is coordinating everyone's schedule so the family can enjoy a meal together. "Our family has a rule: Tuesday and Thursday nights we all eat together," said a mother with three children. "At first it was hard, but now everyone knows the schedule and we enjoy each other's company instead of waving to each other in passing."

Take advantage of being together by planning a few simple activities:

- Assign one family member to place a unique centerpiece on the table each week. One three-year-old, immensely proud of her "own" roll of adhesive tape, spent fifteen minutes looking for the perfect smooth rock. She spent the next twenty minutes tearing pieces of tape and covering the rock to make it smooth and shiny. All week she smiled as people commented on her most unique centerpiece. A budding ballerina, so excited about receiving her first pair of toe shoes, created a stand to display her shoes on the table.

- Write out and fill a container with silly combinations of words. Have combinations such as: "sick polka-dotted snake," "greasy broken pencil," "fluorescent cold liver," or "fuzzy banana." Everyone has to reach in, get a phrase, and use it in a sentence.

- Ask family members to share something they were thankful for today.

- Place a sticker beneath the seat of one chair. That person either gets to choose a family game to play or can stay up past bedtime.
- As you begin eating, set the timer for five minutes. When it goes off, everyone takes his or her plate and moves one chair to the left. This is a simple activity that always produces laughs.

All these ideas require no extra money yet reap extra rewards by creating positive mealtime memories. Make mealtime a time for refueling your body *and* your soul.

> "Better is a dish of vegetables where love is, than a fattened ox and hatred with it."
>
> Proverbs 15:17

Dinner in the Garage

If a tight budget restricts you from eating out, consider making mealtime a unique experience in the comfort of your home. With advance preparation and plenty of creativity, your family can enjoy a memorable meal. Atmosphere is often more important than food itself. A family on a limited budget set aside Friday evening as "Crazy Location Night." The children took turns deciding where the family would eat dinner. A simple meal was prepared and the mystery location was announced with a great flourish: "Tonight, dinner will be eaten in the attic!" announced five-year-old Karen. Everyone then proceeded up the attic steps to eat amidst storage boxes and old high school yearbooks. The following week dinner might be eaten under the kitchen table. Saying grace before dinner takes on a whole new perspective when everyone is gathered for a meal in the bathroom. Neighborhood children began coming on Friday evenings, asking to participate in the mealtime fun. After all, if you were eight years old, wouldn't you think it great fun to eat in the back of a pickup truck parked in the garage on a rainy evening?

Perhaps you'll be lucky and find *yourself* enjoying a meal along with the children. Some other unique places to eat are:

• Around and on your children's swing set.

• One family ate on the flat roof of their garage.

• Take your dinner and sit on your front steps.

If having dinner in your son's bedroom is not your idea of fine dining, do what my friend did. She called and said, "Silvana, I can't do it! Your idea about eating in various locations is too wild for me. But I did find a compromise. Once a week, I let my kids sit at a *different* place at the table. That's as creative as I can get!"

Before you write off the idea, give it a try. You'll be building memories of mealtime fun that will never fade from your children's minds.

Go Ahead, Play With Your Food

How many times have you told your children, "Don't play with your food"? Of course, basic table manners are important, but sometimes shaping and creating food is OK. If a child is recuperating from an illness, or just needs a pick-me-up, try some of these fun adaptations to everyday meals:

• Use a cookie cutter to cut sandwiches into various shapes. Even a boring bologna sandwich takes on new interest when cut in the shape of a heart or gingerbread man.

- Use cookie cutters to cut sliced canned cranberry jelly into amusing shapes.

- Spread peanut butter between two round crackers. Insert six small pretzel sticks into the peanut butter to form the legs of edible bugs.

- Roll a ball of ice cream in shredded coconut. Add raisin or chocolate chip eyes and licorice string whiskers for a shaggy cat.

- Specialty ice cream stores sell ice cream clowns at steep prices. Make your own by placing a round scoop of ice cream on a plate. Top with a pointed ice cream cone for a hat. Decorate the "clown" face with chocolate chips and maraschino cherries. Place cone and ice cream on top of a doughnut representing the clown's collar.

- Serve open-faced hamburgers. Let children squeeze a face or other design on their hamburger with mustard or ketchup.

- Liven up everyday juice by adding ice cubes with fruit chunks frozen inside.

- Decorate plain cookies, cakes, or puddings with chocolate squiggles. Place a handful of chocolate chips in a heavy-duty, reclosable plastic bag. Melt chips in microwave from forty-five to sixty seconds or until chocolate melts. Cut a small corner from the bag and squeeze the chocolate directly onto the cookies or cake. Make random designs, or write chocolate messages.

Messipes: A Microwave Cookbook of Deliciously Messy Masterpieces by Lynn Gordon, Random House.

Togetherness Desserts

Even with an emphasis on low-fat cooking, desserts remain high on most people's list of favorite foods. Instead of making complicated cakes or following time-consuming recipes, work together as a family and use the following no-cook recipes to create desserts:

- Aquarium Pets. Give everyone a clear drinking glass. Place a few grapes (to look like rocks) in the bottom and add a mixture of blueberry Jell-O™. The speed set method using ice cubes works best. After the Jell-O partially sets, push a few gummy fish down into the middle of the glass. Let the Jell-O set and enjoy eating your aquarium.

- Unwrap about twenty-five caramels and place them in a microwave container. Add a few drops of milk and a dab of butter. Microwave for one to two minutes. While this mixture cools, peel and slice apples. Dip the peeled slices of apples into caramel sauce. Lay them on waxed paper to dry.

- Bring out the fondue pot. If you don't have one, check at a local thrift shop or garage sale. Use chocolate pudding for the sauce and dip pieces of fruit and poundcake into it. Start a tradition that if your fruit falls off the fork and into the pudding, you have to do something silly—like sing a song while doing a somersault.

- Lay out graham crackers and make edible greeting cards. Use decorating frosting tubes and write a message on them to give to another family member. What parent wouldn't want to eat a graham cracker decorated by an enthusiastic two year old?

- Fruit kabobs serve two purposes. They are a way to use ripe fruit and they make parents feel good about serving a healthy dessert.

Get everyone involved cutting up apples, bananas, strawberries, and fresh pineapple (if you want to splurge). Push a skewer through fruit and mini-marshmallows, alternating them up the skewer. If your children are young, for safety sake let them poke flat-ended chopsticks through their fruit rather than the sharp, pointed skewers.

Super Kisses and Pretzels

Cooking dinner together is a wonderful time for both sharing the day's events and for learning valuable kitchen skills. Since younger children get frustrated with complicated recipes, it's best to choose recipes that produce quick results. The "Super Kiss" is guaranteed to be a hit with your family, or your family can give them as gifts.

This recipe creates giant crispy cereal treats in the shape of the famous Hershey Kiss.

"Super Kiss" Ingredients

1/4 cup margarine or butter
(1) 10-ounce package marshmallows (about 50) or 4 cups miniature marshmallows
5 cups crispy rice cereal or chocolate crispy rice cereal

Directions

Melt margarine or butter in large saucepan over low heat. Add marshmallows and stir until completely melted. Stirring constantly, cook 3 minutes longer over low heat. Remove from heat. Add cereal and stir until well coated. Cool slightly, but not completely. Butter your fingers. Press warm mixture into large, buttered funnels. When cool, unmold from funnel and wrap in plastic. Wrap in tin foil and make a white tag to stick out the top of the kiss that says "Super Kiss." Makes 2 to 4 large kisses.

For something a bit less sweet, try making a batch of pretzel dough. Everyone can mold and shape the dough into a unique, baked creation.

Soft Pretzels

1 package active dry yeast
1-1/2 cups lukewarm water
1 teaspoon salt
3 teaspoons sugar
4 cups flour
1 egg, beaten

Directions

Dissolve yeast in water; add salt, sugar, and flour. Knead 5-10 minutes, and add more flour as necessary to reduce stickiness. Twist dough into shape of cars, trucks, airplanes, animals, flowers, trees, gingerbread boys, numerals, or circles. Place on Teflon baking sheet. Brush with beaten egg. Bake at 425° for 15 minutes or until lightly browned.

Sensational Snacks

"Mom, I'm hungry," cries a plaintive voice, only twenty-five minutes after dinner. Let's face it, children need to eat more often than adults. In addition to keeping a handy supply of fruits and vegetables available, encourage children to make their own snacks.

Snacks provide the opportunity to experiment with a small amount of food. Children learn to combine items into new taste sensations, even if they are the only ones brave enough to eat the culinary delights.

The following snack suggestions are "idea starters" to help children develop their own specialty of the house:

- Make your own brand of trail mix by combining odds and ends from the cupboard. Mix popped popcorn, raisins, fish crackers, and chocolate chips to get a combination unavailable in stores.

- Almost any food tastes better dipped in chocolate! Melt a handful of chocolate chips in the microwave and dip pretzels, apple slices, or vanilla wafers.

- Under adult supervision, make fruit smoothies in the blender. Experiment with various combinations of fruit, crushed ice, fruit juice, and ice cream.

- Spread a small amount of whipped topping between two animal crackers. Freeze for twenty to thirty minutes. Create a variation by slightly softening ice cream, spreading it between the animal crackers, and then freezing them for mini ice cream sandwiches.

- Add your own flavors to a bowl of yogurt. Try a drop of vanilla and cinnamon, or even a spoonful of salsa.

- Grate cheese over flour or corn tortillas. Add tomato slices, shredded carrot, or sour cream. Wrap in paper towel and microwave for fourteen to twenty seconds.
  Don't forget to clean up the mess!

Creative
Games
for the
Family

Hunting for Anything

We're all familiar with Easter Egg hunts and the excitement at finding colorful dyed treasures. When our daughter was three, she loved finding the eggs so much that we had five egg hunts on Easter—and two to three daily for the rest of the week. She was thrilled to look for plastic eggs over and over and over!

Since children enjoy "the hunt" so much, try a peanut hunt anytime of the year. Simply hide peanuts (in the shell) throughout the house or outdoors. If you have younger children who can't find peanuts as fast as older siblings, mark ten to fifteen peanuts with a felt-tipped marker or tie yarn around them. These peanuts are off limits to older children, so that little ones find the peanuts at their own speed.

Give your children a bag and let them hunt for the following items:

- "Little People" that you have distributed throughout the house.
- Styrofoam packing peanuts. Reuse by hiding them.
- Wrapped Halloween candy your children have collected. Have your candy hunt in November.

Once a year, one family with four children has their "Annual Candy Hunt" on January 12. It's something to look forward to after the holiday rush subsides. Wrapped candy is hidden in every possible nook and cranny of the house. Because the pace to find as much candy as possible becomes frantic, there's one rule: you have to leave an area the same way you found it. This prevents bureau drawers left open, bookcases emptied of books—well, you get the picture. Part of the fun is not finding candy during the hunt and discovering it in obscure places for the next several weeks.

Another family so enjoyed their hunts, they even included the family dog by hiding small dog biscuits in locations he could reach.

> "There will always be worthwhile causes, but not always a two year old in your lap."
>
> Freda Ingle Briggs

Return to the Classics

Your children probably maneuver on the Internet with ease and have little fear of the new math. But can they handle classic activities like dominoes, jacks, and pick-up sticks? In our fast paced society with its emphasis on speed and technology, we need to find time to share some old-time favorites.

Pick-up sticks require concentration and a steady hand. Since the ends are pointed, keep them away from younger children. If you don't have manufactured pick-up sticks, substitute bread sticks, pretzel rods, or pixie sticks. The idea remains the same—pick up one stick without disturbing the others in the pile.

- Card houses entertain children of all ages. Bring out a deck of cards and use four to build a base, add a roof, and continue as high as possible.
- Black and white domino chips are a familiar sight in many homes. After playing a traditional domino game, line them up

vertically, one inch apart. Give the first one a push and see what happens. Spread a graham cracker with peanut butter or chocolate frosting. Make edible dominoes by adding chocolate chips to make "dots."

• Get out the newspapers and make old-fashioned, three-cornered paper hats. If you tire of making those, place two to three sheets of newsprint over your child's head. Wrap several strips of masking tape around the newspaper and the crown of his or her head. Roll the edges of the newspaper upwards or trim the edges to make a floppy brim.

Just in case you run out of ideas, try rock-scissors-paper, thumb wrestling, jacks, matchbox car races, hangman, and paper doll chains. Who said fun has to be high-tech?

> *The Great American Book of Sidewalk, Stoop, Dirt, Curb, and Alley Games* by Fred Ferritti, Workman.
> *Rainy Day Pastimes: 215 Ideas to Keep Children Happy* by Magda Gray, Cavendish Publishing.

Crazy Olympics

Olympic fever hits the country every four years as we watch well-trained athletes compete in a variety of sporting events. Since most of us can only dream of running, flipping, and diving like an Olympic athlete, the next best thing is to participate in a "Crazy Olympic" event. Invite friends over, or just participate as a family in this low-key event.

The fun of Crazy Olympics is that everyone is on an equal basis.

Preschoolers compete with older siblings, parents challenge teens, and everyone has fun.

To plan a Crazy Olympic event, walk through the house and see what kind of things you could use for an event. Some suggestions include:

- Javelin Throw: Contestants see how far they can throw a straw. Give extra points for dramatic grunts and groans as they toss the javelin.
- Discus Throw: Have the youngest family member decorate a few white paper plates. Measure who can throw the paper discus the farthest. For variety, record who throws it the highest or the straightest.
- Hurdles: Lay out several pillows or couch cushions on the floor. Participants race toward a finish line—crawling and "jumping" over the hurdles.
- Fifty-Yard Dash: Participants run as fast as they can to the finish line with a partially inflated beach ball between their legs.
- Standing Broad Grin: Measure everyone for the biggest smile.
- Shot Put: Yes, you can do a shot put in the house—if you use cotton balls.

After all the crazy events, be sure to give awards. Attach a ribbon to empty juice can lids for instant Gold Medal winners.

The Working Scavenger Hunt

Remember how, as a child, you eagerly held the list of items you needed to find on a scavenger hunt? Then you raced as fast as possible, looking to find that elusive round rock or purple shoelace.

Family scavenger hunts provide a great opportunity for physical and mental exercise. To make the hunt safe and fair, consider a few guidelines:

- Match nonreaders with an older partner, or give pictures of the items to be found.
- The location from where you take the item must be left as you found it. (Close drawers, return items to shelves, etc.)
- Set specific boundaries. Can you go next door to a neighbor? Must you stay inside the house? Is the garage off limits?

Include on the list some items that involve creativity such as "write a poem about a family member" or "draw what you want for your birthday."

One family incorporated a scavenger hunt and household chores. In addition to finding items such as a baby picture of Dad, an old toothbrush, and a used piece of duct tape, the parents cleverly included the following items:

- Dust the top of your dresser and bring us the used dust cloth.
- Rake up a pile of leaves from the front yard and bring us the bag full of leaves.
- Sweep the front porch steps and bring us the dirt in a bag.
- Draw a Happy Birthday card for Grandma.
- Sort out your sock drawer and have Mom or Dad "inspect" it.
- Pick some flowers from the garden, put them in a vase, and display them somewhere in the house.

What a great way to get a few chores completed without anyone complaining!

Birthday Bashes

In some communities, one set of parents attempts to outdo other parents in planning extravaganzas to celebrate children's birthdays. Professional clowns, gourmet foods, and, of course, expensive gifts soon come to be expected, even by preschoolers. Naturally, we want our children to feel special on their birthday, but there are ways to achieve that goal without having to take out a loan.

Pat Boone, in an interview about his family traditions, shared an unconventional idea. When one of his family members had a birthday, they *gave* presents to everyone else. It was a way of showing they were glad to be part of the Boone family. If that is too extreme for your child, here are some other ways to celebrate:

- Instead of a big party, ask your children about a new experience they'd like to try with a few friends. Maybe the circus is coming to town, or you could take them to a professional sporting event.
- If your child wants a traditional party, hire a college student majoring in recreation or education to help out. For a minimal amount, a student is happy to share experience in games, crafts, or storytelling.
- Brainstorm with your children about some unusual activities they could do. One eight year old was thrilled to go out for ice cream with four friends and then visit "The Dollar Store." Each girl received one dollar and could buy whatever she wanted. (Can you imagine what it would be like to go in a store and be told, "You can buy *anything* in this store"?)
- Have your child select a book and donate it to the school library on his or her birthday. Include a book plate in the front recognizing your child as the book donor.

- One family decided expensive gifts were not part of their values. Now when someone has a birthday, they ask friends to bring donations of canned food to the party. The birthday child gets a simple celebration and the local food bank get the food.

Birthday Express is a catalog full of decorations and supplies for children's birthdays. 1-800-424-7843.

Pin the Tail on the Donkey and Other Party Games by Joanna Cole and Stephanie Calmenson, Morrow Junior Books.

Surrounded By Beauty (And a Mess)

Several years ago, I visited a Christian home in an upper-class neighborhood. Neat hedges bordered the front lawn, and an expensive-looking wreath decorated the front door. Inside, the house looked like a model home, complete with coordinated curtains and pillows. A quick tour through the house showed little evidence that people actually lived there. Even the two girls' rooms had perfectly made beds without a single dirty sock on the floor.

The house looked ready for a *Better Homes and Gardens* photo shoot but showed little signs of creativity. The refrigerator was even devoid of any school artwork! As the girls arrived home from school, they were told to hang their backpacks in the closet and watch television. "If they're watching TV, they don't get the house messy," explained their mother.

When God put Adam and Eve in the garden, he surrounded

them with flowers, birds, lakes, and other natural beauty. God gave Moses directions for building a marvelous tabernacle. People wove linens and embroidered them, designed robes for priests, and made jewelry. Later in the Bible, the woman described in Proverbs 31 used scarlet and purple materials to clothe her family. All of these examples give evidence that God enjoys our creative expressions.

Martha Stewart probably won't feature the following ideas on her TV show, but they demonstrate that creative efforts are acknowledged and appreciated in your family.

- Before dinner, have everyone fold his or her napkin into a unique animal or shape.
- String a thin rope across the living room wall. Use clothespins to attach and display school art projects.
- Ask the youngest family member to make up a song to sing about your family.
- Read the Bible from a version you normally don't use.
- Use the bathroom mirror to write notes to family members with felt-tip markers.

> "One of the advantages of being disorderly is that one is constantly making exciting new discoveries."
>
> A.A. Milne

Indoor Games

If it's either too hot or too cold to go outdoors and everyone is tired of quiet board games, move back the furniture and enjoy some wild and crazy indoor games:

- Tape a ruler or wooden spoon to the back of a paper plate to form a racket. String a piece of yarn from one side of the room to the other, about four feet off the ground. Play indoor badminton using a balloon and your paper plate rackets.

- Substitute bubbles for the balloon and try to fan the bubbles over the piece of yarn.

- Glue two plastic cereal-size bowls together, bottom to bottom. Attach a piece of elastic or ribbon to one bowl to help keep it on your head. Yes, you will look silly wearing a double bowl! Choose a partner and toss a light bean bag or some kind of very soft ball (perhaps made from yarn) into the air. Watch your partner maneuver to try to catch the ball with their head bowl.

- This game leaves the house messy but provides fun and a great photo opportunity. Divide the family into two teams. Designate an adult to be the announcer. This person describes what he or she is looking for. "I'm looking for a person wearing three pairs of socks, a purple shirt, and green hair bow that is holding a dog bone and an old homework assignment." Each team races to dress up one of their team members exactly as the announcer described.

- Find two empty one-gallon milk jugs. Have an adult cut them in half. (For added safety, put a strip of masking tape over the cut half with the handle.) These two "scoops" are great for tossing balls or bean bags back and forth. Give older children Ping-Pong balls to toss. This is a bit more difficult as they need to adjust their movements to avoid the balls bouncing back out.

- Play musical chairs differently. Here's how: Instead of eliminating people who don't find a chair, remove a chair each round. Then watch as children sit on each other's lap when the music stops. If younger children play, substitute couch cushions for chairs to avoid five people sitting on one chair, falling off, and getting hurt.

More Indoor Fun

Who says hopscotch is only for the playground? Use masking tape to form the hopscotch squares on the carpet. If a basement or rec room has a cement floor, use chalk for the outline.

- Find a blank wall in your house and shine your slide projector light on it. Let children make shadows with their hands and bodies.

- Clear some space and bring out the jump ropes. Can adults jump at triple speed to do "Hot Peppers"? This activity takes little space and burns off energy. If you can't remember jump rope jingles, check out *Anna Banana: 101 Jump Rope Rhymes* by Joanna Cole and Alan Tiegreen, Morrow Junior Books.

- Give children construction paper, and ask them to decorate and cut out twelve paper fish. Slip a paper clip onto the fish mouth. Randomly place the fish on the floor, inside a hula hoop (to designate a pond). Make a fishing pole with a stick, string, and a magnet for the hook. Let children attempt to "hook" their fish. Increase the challenge by fishing while hopping on one leg, holding the pole in your mouth, or fishing while continuously walking outside the hula hoop.

- Since you already have your hula hoop out, get moving! Count who can keep the hoop on their hips the longest. Who can keep it going around their neck?

- Give each child a piece of paper and a crayon without the paper wrapper. Set the timer for five minutes and have everyone make at least five rubbings of items in the house. Simply place the paper over an item and rub with the flat side of the crayon for a distinctive design. Try to guess what people used to achieve their rubbing.

- Set up ten empty milk jugs or pop bottles. Roll a ball and try to knock down as many as possible.

> Focus on the Family offers two magazines for children filled with game and craft ideas:
> *Clubhouse Junior* for four to eight year olds.
> *Clubhouse* for eight to twelve year olds. 1-800-232-6459.

Rainy Day Fun

Try some of these easy-to-do activities when you're all stuck indoors together:

- Practice hanging spoons from your nose.
- Try juggling scarves, shoes, balloons, and eggs (just kidding).
- Have a paper airplane-throwing contest.
- Compete in thumb wrestling.
- Shake whipping cream to make butter.
- Do self-portraits by looking into a mirror.
- Draw a map of your neighborhood.
- Make origami figures without a pattern.
- Make origami figures *with* a pattern!

- Hold markers between your toes and color.
- Play Twenty Questions or Animal, Vegetable, or Mineral.
- Draw a picture of a machine that could tie shoes.
- Draw a picture of how you'll look in ten years.
- Clean out a closet together.
- Read by candlelight at night.
- Practice a family cheer with crazy motions.
- Bake bread.
- Play charades.
- Draw the ideal school classroom.
- Create a family comic strip.
- Make a model of a new carnival ride.
- Write a letter to your favorite author.

> *The Address Book of Children's Authors and Illustrators:*
> over 100 addresses and background information
> included. Available from T.S. Denison Publishing.

Beyond Board Games

Sometimes ordinary activities take on new significance when they are enjoyed with friends. (It must be the same principle that transforms your children into charming, polite, well-behaved children when they visit friends.)

For an easy get-together, invite friends to bring board games for an afternoon of fun. Doesn't sound too exciting? Just wait!

Try some variations on a traditional game of checkers or Clue with these ideas:

- Relay Races: Set up four copies of the same game on four tables. Four families line up at an equal distance from the tables. At the starting whistle, the first players in each line run up to the table, roll the dice, move their pieces, then run back and tag the next family player. Repeat until there's a winner. (This activity works well with puzzles in place of games.) Hint: Use simple family games—not Monopoly.

- Toes Only! Remember those board games with the tricky spinners? Well, add more interest by having all players take off their shoes and socks and play a whole game spinning only with their toes. Guaranteed laughs! Hint: Rolling dice with toes might work for teens and up, but it can be frustrating for younger children.

- Musical Games: Set up five tables with the same game. Families play for fifteen minutes (or some other brief period of time). When you ring a bell, all players move to the same position at the next table.

- Speed It Up! All players play as fast as possible, trying to get the game done within ten minutes. In family recreation, it doesn't matter so much who wins or loses—players love the sheer comedy of moving so quickly.

The "New Ungame" is now available at most toy stores and Christian bookstores. This non-competitive game offers no winners or losers. It does offer the chance to develop light-hearted communication skills.

Crafts **With More Creativity and Fewer Directions**

Decorated Underwear

"**W**ho, me? Do arts and crafts projects? Never!" Even if you think you can't paint or create a sculpture, arts and crafts activities provide a wonderful outlet for wild and unorthodox thinking. Unfortunately, many school art projects insist on conformity and exact cutting, gluing, and coloring. Let children get creative and messy by experimenting with mixing paint or blending their own play dough. As children feel free to design their own masterpieces, they gain self-confidence that transfers to other areas of life.

- Get the whole family together to create a wood sculpture made from discarded wood scraps available from a cabinetmaker.

- Buy fabric paint and decorate T-shirts. One family got so carried away with their artistic endeavors they decorated their underwear!

- Try making sculptures from marshmallows and uncooked spaghetti.

- Have a newspaper fashion show. Using only tape and newspaper, design outfits ranging from swimsuits to wedding gowns.

- Drop a marble into a container of paint. Remove with a spoon and drop into an empty shoe box. Shake the box to make a colorful spider web effect.

- Cut paper into small random shapes. Glue onto background paper for a mosaic picture.

- Give children plain white coffee filters. Add a few drops of food coloring to a small container of water. Children enjoy painting the coffee filters with the colored water. Colors blend and swirl to create a rainbow effect.

The process of experimenting when there are no set rules gives children experience in decision making. They have a goal of making a project, and it's up to them to try various techniques of mixing paint, adding sequins, or shaping clay. If the result isn't what they expected, they still understand the process and can make adaptations next time. Having fun together and laughing at unique creations is more important than mastering a perfect painting.

Kool-Aid Play Dough

Mix 1 cup sifted flour, 1/2 cup salt, 3 tablespoons oil, and 1 small package of Kool-Aid or other unsweetened powdered drink. Add 1 cup boiling water. Stir the ingredients together, and knead mixture until it forms a soft dough. Store in covered container.

Free Art Supplies

Children love to create art projects, especially when they don't have to follow a set of complicated instructions. Unfortunately, many school and church projects encourage conformity, requiring identical cotton-ball snowmen.

Provide children with an assortment of art supplies and no instructions to encourage creativity and problem solving. How can they glue a plastic lid on top of the aluminum foil ball? How can they keep their paper sculpture from collapsing?

Craft and art supplies can be expensive, so here are some ways to cut down on the expense:

- Check with home-decorating stores for free, outdated wallpaper books. The large pages are ideal for wrapping gifts, decorating doll houses, and designing stationery.

- Many cabinetmakers and furniture builders have small wood scraps in various shapes they are willing to let you have. These are perfect for creative wood sculptures.

- Printing shops have a steady supply of paper scraps available in various shapes, colors, and textures. Children can create bookmarks and paper sculptures or just cut and color.

- Upholstery shops or custom fabric stores have out-of-date fabric samples to give away. Use them for doll clothes, collages, and more.

- Newspaper offices often have leftover ends of plain newsprint rolls for free or at a nominal cost. Most rolls are twenty to twenty-five feet long and wide enough for large murals, body tracings, and any giant-size art project.

- Ask photographers for used cardboard frames and empty film canisters.

Lick and Stick

You have to try this to understand the fun. Obtain biodegradable packing peanuts made from cornstarch. Simply lick one piece and, like magic, it attaches to another piece. Great for making igloos and other unique sculptures.

Chopsticks and Astroturf Plugs

P arents need more than a sense of humor and a ton of patience to get through a day. If you've been cooped up because of chicken pox or inclement weather, it might be time to bring out the "WHAT IS IT?" box. This box goes beyond the traditional craft supplies like scissors, glue, and scrap paper. Keep this box full of unusual items such as: Velcro, unused chopsticks, and empty film canisters. Then get really wild and order some items from the Creative Educational Surplus Catalog (1-800-886-6428) at reasonable prices. You'll be able to get wonderful imagination-stretchers, such as:

- Giant forty-three-inch paper bags
- Various sizes of lamb's wool
- Astroturf plugs
- Giant eyedroppers, and even
- Oddball-shaped funnels.

A "WHAT IS IT?" box forces you to keep your eye open for unusual items to put into the box, as well as giving children the opportunity to create something with no specific end product in mind out of the box. Our daughter spends hours in the bathtub with several plastic containers full of colored water, mixing concoctions with her giant eyedroppers. Other children use the strange items to set up a "Weird and Strange Museum," charging admission to see the unique exhibits. Some children incorporate all the items in the box to set up a Rube Goldberg-type machine with levers and pulleys.

Start collecting all the unique items you can, so that, on those days when all else fails, you can pull out the special box and have your children ask, "What is this?"

- Take a plastic gallon milk jug and cut a four-inch square out of one side. Let children transform the jug into a doll house or fire station. Decorate with markers and construction paper windows. Put "Little People" inside. Cut a scrap of felt into a five-inch by seven-inch rectangle. Cut a one-inch hole in the center. Decorate with scrap material, buttons, and sequins to make a doorknob decoration.

> *Creative Educational Surplus* offers a free catalog listing unique educational items. 1-800-886-6428. Supplies are often limited, so order soon after receiving the catalog.

Homemade Chalk

laying with chalk (other than scraping your fingernails across a chalkboard) is a favorite activity. Show your children how easily they can make their own chalk.

Save the plastic trays that store manicotti shells. These form the molds for homemade chalk. Put 3/4 cup water in a disposable container. Slowly stir in about 1-1/2 cups of plaster of Paris. Add a few drops of food coloring. Mixture should be thick but not clumpy. Pour mixture into manicotti tray, and tap several times to release air bubbles. Let dry for at least forty-eight hours and you'll have a set of custom-made chalk. (In place of a manicotti tray, wrap wax paper on the inside of a three-inch cardboard tube, and duct tape one end. Pour plaster into tube and let dry as above.)

Now that you have all this chalk, purchase blackboard paint and paint a door or wall for an instant chalkboard.

- In chalk on the garage floor, create a bird's-eye view of your house or neighborhood.

- Mix up several batches of chalk, wrap with a bow, and give as a gift. Include the directions so the recipient can make their own.

- If you really want to make authentic chalk, crush six egg shells until you have a fine powder. Add 1 teaspoon flour and 1 teaspoon very hot water. Mix well and place in mold. Let dry at least four days.

- Since you probably have leftover plaster of Paris after making chalk, use it to create free-form sculptures. Measure 4 tablespoons of water and 8 tablespoons of plaster of Paris into a lock top plastic bag. Mixture should be like a soft play dough. Squeeze the bag to create a free-form sculpture. After you get the shape you want, hold bag in one position for two to three minutes. As the plaster hardens, remove the bag and paint the dry sculpture.

Words From Nowhere

We all know the best way to get a child's attention is to whisper something to a spouse or friend. Children love secrets, written or verbal. Look at the popularity of the "telephone" game where each person whispers the same phrase to another person and then another and another.

Secret writing is a novel way to help children's writing skills while satisfying their desire to share a secret.

- Invisible ink is easy to make and gives dramatic results. Squeeze the juice of a lemon into a cup. (Roll the lemon firmly over a table several times to release the most juice.) Using a cotton swab, write a message on a piece of paper with the lemon juice. Let the juice dry completely before moving the paper. Give the secret message to someone else. Under adult supervision, hold the paper close to a heat source such as a light bulb, toaster, or radiator. The message soon appears in light brown letters.

- Backward writing is easier to read than it is to write. Simply hold in front of a mirror to decipher the message. To write the backward words, hold a stiff piece of paper to your chest. Looking only in the mirror, write a message on paper. Some children find it easier to use all capital letters.

- Use a white crayon or candle to write the message on white paper. The wax of the candle or crayons resists moisture. To make the message appear, paint over the entire page with watercolors.

- Inflate a balloon and write a message on it with permanent markers. Release the air, and give the balloon to a child in a lunch box, or place it on a pillow. They will enjoy inflating the balloon to read the message.

Gifts From the Heart

Holidays, birthdays, and special "I think you're great" days all give us the opportunity to give gifts. Instead of rushing to the mall to buy Dad a necktie or Aunt Maxine some perfume, have your children assist you in creating personalized, unique gifts.

- Create a scrapbook for the lucky recipient. Collect photographs, jokes, and magazine articles related to the person's interests. Assemble them into a scrapbook or photo album. One family made a scrapbook for their grandfather who loved antique cars. It included magazine pictures, a poem about Grandpa, and a cover drawing of him sitting in a Model A Duesenberg.

- Give the person a coupon book for age-appropriate gifts. A busy mother would love two hours of free baby-sitting while Grandma could redeem a coupon for someone to mow her lawn and then to eat cookies together afterwards. If you really want to make a special gift, give certificates for the "Gift-of-the-Month" club. Recipients can look forward to a small gift monthly for the rest of the year.

- Collect favorite recipes from family members. Type them up and ask children to add their artwork. Make copies and distribute to everyone that contributed a recipe. Watch out, Betty Crocker!

- Check out specialty catalogs to find gifts pertaining to the person's interest. A left-handed person appreciated potato peelers and scissors designed for lefties. If there's a quilter on your gift list, order an item from one of the many quilting catalogs.

For a directory of specialized catalogs, contact: *World Famous Catalogs,* 951 Broken Sound Parkway NW, Building 190, Boca Raton, FL 33431-0857.

Stamps Galore

Creating art projects using rubber stamps is popular for all ages. Entire stores devote themselves to selling ornate (and expensive) stamps. Rather than blowing your budget purchasing stamps, consider making your own. One of the easiest ways uses foam innersoles. These thin foam pads lend themselves to a variety of shapes and sizes. Best of all, even young children can cut the foam.

- Purchase a generic brand of men's extra-large innersoles. (The price is the same as for small, so get the larger size.)
- Help children cut out basic shapes such as hearts or stars. After they get the feel of cutting the foam, encourage more detailed designs.
- Glue the foam shapes onto a block of wood. (If wood is unavailable, use clean, all-one-piece jar lids as a base for the stamp.)
- Let the glue dry thoroughly and begin stamping! For best results, use washable ink pads. Many stores sell ink pads in silver, gold, or rainbow colors.

Innersoles make ideal stamps because of the easy-to-cut, non-messy foam. For variety, try making stamps out of these items:

- Purchase a square art eraser and cut a design on the top.
- Cut small shapes out of a Styrofoam meat tray. Glue shapes onto a block of wood and use as a stamp.
- Ordinary kitchen sponges, cut into unusual shapes, make great stamps.
- If you have a small piece of self-adhesive weather stripping, cut the foam into shapes, peel off the paper covering the adhesive, and attach the forms to wood.

> *The Stamp-Pad Printing Book* by Florence Pellit, Thomas Crowell Publishing.
>
> Four complete stamping activity kits are available at Christian bookstores or from Revelation International. They include stamps, stencils, and paper with the themes of Jonah and the whale, David and Goliath, Esther the Queen, and Noah's Ark.

Homemade Fun

We all know that toddlers enjoy playing with gift boxes more than the gifts themselves. Capitalize on children's imaginations by providing them with opportunities to create their own handmade toys.

- If you have the ability to transport large objects, obtain several empty refrigerator boxes from appliance stores. They make great playhouses or tunnels. Provide paint and brushes outdoors and let children decorate to their hearts' content without fear of making a mess.

- Cut two inches off the top of several half-gallon milk cartons. Force one carton inside another to form a sturdy block. The blocks create the basis for a variety of building structures. Cover with adhesive-backed paper for a more finished look.

- If you're at the beach, it's easy to set up a sand-bowling game. Using empty cups or buckets as forms, create sand "bowling pins." Roll a beach ball and try to knock over the "sand pins."

- Two paper plates stapled together (so they make a dome) turn into indoor Frisbees. Decorate with markers and crayons. Designate a box or hula hoop as a target, and try to hit the designated target.

- Ever go to an ice cream parlor and get your sundae served in a plastic boat-shaped container? Take these home for bath toys or use them in outdoor swimming pools. Float the boats in a sink full of water and estimate how many pennies it takes to sink the boat.

As children see hundreds of ads for expensive electronic toys, it's a good idea to teach them about homemade fun. When my daughter wanted a pink plastic convertible for her dolls, my husband took her to his workshop. Two hours later they emerged with a wooden car that looks nothing like what's advertised in a toy catalog, but has brought hours of fun to our daughter.

> "Every child is an artist. The problem is how to remain an artist once he grows up."
>
> Pablo Picasso

Junior Michelangelos

Ah! The wonders of working with paint! It stains clothes, gets under fingernails, and colors carpets. Yet no other medium lends itself to such wide opportunities for creative expression. One kindergarten teacher told about studying the Sistine Chapel with her class. (How's that for creativity?) They discussed Michelangelo's persistence in painting while lying on his back. To demonstrate this point, the children donned smocks and sunglasses (to avoid paint in their eyes), and proceeded to lie on the floor. Their task? Paint pictures on the undersides of all the school tables. While you may not want children to paint the ceilings in your home, here are some ways to inspire budding artists:

- Mix two to three teaspoons of salt into a container of paint. When the picture dries, the salt hardens and creates wonderful three-dimensional paintings.

- Hang up a plain-colored sheet or tablecloth. Collect several pump-type spray bottles—the kind used to mist plants. Fill half-full with water and add a few drops of paint. The mixture needs to remain thin in order not to clog the sprayer. Let children experiment on adjusting the spray control nozzle to create a fine burst of color on the cloth or a steady spray.

- Create your own Rorsharch prints. Fold a piece of paper in half, then open it. Dip a piece of string into paint and drape it on one side of the paper. For best results, curl the string in a free form pattern. Fold the paper and hold it down. Then pull the string out to create a mirror-image abstract painting.
- Pour a few drops of liquid starch onto paper. Add one or more colors of paint for a swirled effect.

For a new painting experience, order BioColor from Discount School Supply (1-800-627-2829). BioColor replaces tempera paint. It's washable, can be used for face paint, and even makes homemade stickers.

More Paint Projects

Young artists still want more paint projects? Try these ideas:
- Add glitter to your wet painting for a sparkling effect.
- Hold a leaf by its stem on a piece of newspaper. Use a brush to cover the leaf with paint. Place the leaf on a white piece of paper, paint side down. Cover with lightweight cardboard and rub to create a genuine leaf print.
- Cut a snowflake design like children make at Christmas. Tape edges on a piece of construction paper. Paint over the snowflake. Gently remove tape and snowflake for an intricate painted design.
- Mix three to four teaspoons of liquid dishwashing soap into a cup of liquid tempera paint. Give each child a straw and tell him

or her to blow into the paint mixture until bubbles spill over the top of the container. Then place a piece of paper on top of the bubbles. The bubbles will burst and leave unique designs on the paper.

- If you are really brave, let children finger-paint on a table top. When they have a picture or design they like, cover it with a piece of paper. Rub the back and remove to show a reverse print from the table-top design.

- Drop three to four teaspoons of thin, liquid tempera paint on a piece of paper. Use a straw to blow the paint across the paper for unique designs. Have the children experiment with different angles of the straw to obtain the best results.

- Mix a thin batch of tempera paint and pour into ice cube trays. Stick a wooden stick into each cube. When the paint freezes, have children paint with frozen ice cubes. Make sure younger children know these are not Popsicles.

- Place 1/4 cup liquid laundry starch with 3 tablespoons powered tempera paint in a lock-top plastic bag. Close the bag, making sure to squeeze out air. Cover the seal with masking tape and let the children make their own self-contained pictures.

Designer Pillowcases

Grandparents and relatives love receiving homemade gifts from children. Yet it's often difficult to find a craft project that children can make by themselves and that can still be recognizable to give as a gift.

Children four years and older can easily make designer pillowcases as gifts or to use themselves. Begin with a washed, solid-colored pillowcase. Some craft books suggest using fabric crayons directly on the material. An easier method is purchasing fabric crayons designed to use on *paper*. Let children experiment with various designs and patterns. Drawing on paper allows room for mistakes or various adaptations. (Remind your child that all writing must be in a mirror image in order to be readable when transferred to the pillowcase.)

When your child is satisfied with his or her picture, simply follow the directions on the box of fabric crayons. It's as simple as placing the paper drawing face down on the pillowcase. Use a piece of cardboard between the ironing board cover and the pillowcase to stop the color from bleeding through.

Gently press down with a hot iron for about forty-five seconds. Do not iron back and forth, since this will smear the picture. Keep pressing until the design transfers to the fabric. Remove the paper and use a black fabric pen to outline the picture on the pillowcase.

Some variations:

- Purchase solid-colored pillowcases at garage sales. Let children decorate them as a slumber party activity.
- Use the same fabric crayons to create one-of-a-kind T-shirts.
- Purchase a large, white tablecloth. Every year on your child's birthday, have him or her draw and date a picture. Use this birthday tablecloth as a record of your child's artistic development.

Artwork Galore

Any parent with school-aged children faces the same task: What to do with the assortment of artistic creations that come home daily? Large sheets of finger-painted pictures and intricate construction paper mosaics represent our children's time and effort that we hate to throw away. Recycle their artwork by some of the following ideas:

- Use colorful drawings and paintings as wrapping paper for gifts.
- Paste artwork on a twelve-by-eighteen-inch piece of cardboard. Cover with clear adhesive paper or have the piece laminated for personalized placemats.
- Photocopy a year's worth of calendar pages. Match a piece of your child's artwork with a page of a monthly calendar. Attach to construction paper. Punch holes in all twelve pages and use string or plain key rings to form a binding you can flip open to each month. Grandparents love to receive their one-of-a-kind yearly calendar.
- Collect all the papers for one month. On the last day of the month, have your child select a favorite. On New Year's Day, bring out the twelve pieces of artwork and narrow down the selection of favorites to one. That honored piece gets professionally framed and hung in a place of honor.
- Sponsor an art auction. Invite relatives and close friends over to view a display of your children's artwork. Before the bidding starts, invite the children to give brief explanations of their projects, telling what type of paint was used, why they chose the color of paper they chose, if they used any unusual tools to make the art piece, and so forth. Select an auctioneer to begin the bidding at ten cents for each masterpiece. Set a limit of one dollar to keep costs manageable. Your children will earn a bit of money, and you will have less "artwork" in the house!
- When all else fails, purchase extra-strength magnets to hold up all the artwork covering your refrigerator!

Collecting Bugs

Children have a natural tendency to collect items. A collection states, "This is a part of me. This is what I'm interested in." Young children delight in collecting small twigs, broken seashells, rocks, and even leaves. One budding naturalist divided her leaf collection into two types: those with bugs and those without.

- Encourage every family member to start a collection. Maybe your own collection of real antique sports cars is non-existent, but you could collect *model* sports cars.

- Help children display their collections. An offer to build a shelf or buy a scrapbook shows your interest. Hang a hammock in the corner of a room as a place to store and display stuffed animals. Dedicate a shelf on your china cabinet for your child's ceramic frogs.

- Check out library books on children's collections. A reference book on stamp identification or the history of coin collecting encourages both reading and research.

- Don't be upset if children lose interest in one collection and take up another. This is a normal part of child development. One young stamp collector became intrigued with stamps depicting castles. This led to a whole new interest in building and collecting model castles. The stamp collection remained in the closet.

- Expand on your children's interests. If they collect horse statues, visit a riding stable. Find an adult in the community with a similar collection and arrange for a visit. See if a local hobby group meets in your area. Ask if your child is welcome to attend one of their meetings.

- Give your children supplies for labeling and identifying their collections. Label makers, computer-generated signs, or handwritten poster board drawings make the collection look "official."

Memories and collections go together. The shell you picked up on your first visit to the beach, or the doll passed on to you from a dear relative carries emotional attachments. Encourage children to relive memories through a collection.

Marking the Spot

As children read books, they frequently need to mark their place. Instead of folding down a page corner or sticking a pencil in the book to show where they left off, help them make personalized bookmarks. These also make practical gifts for other readers.

Construction paper or lightweight cardboard makes the best backing. The backsides of old greeting cards work well, also. Cut the paper to the size you need, usually about six to eight inches long and two to three inches wide. Set out a wide assortment of craft items and let the bookmark party begin.

- Ordinary pinking shears give bookmark edges a distinctive touch. Many craft stores carry children's scissors which cut in wavy or zigzag patterns.

- Use up all the assorted stickers in your house to decorate a book-mark. Use markers to add details or backgrounds to the stickers.

- Have any photographs with people squinting or yawning? Cut them up, glue to the bookmark's background and add silly captions.

- Draw a picture of yourself reading a book.

- Decoupaged bookmarks are shiny and durable. After drawing or pasting pictures on the cardboard, mix a solution of 1/2 cup glue and 1/4 cup water. Brush over the bookmark. Let dry. (Don't worry about the way it looks—it dries clear.) Repeat several times.

- Cut out magazine pictures and decorate with your favorite animals, food, or activities.
- Cut scraps of wrapping paper in unusual shapes and glue down to make colorful designs.

One family got so carried away making bookmarks, they ended up with twenty-five! After keeping some for their own use, they donated the rest to the school library.

Kits for Kids

Gift shops and designer boutiques offer a variety of pre-packaged, elegantly wrapped baskets full of bath items or gourmet cooking utensils. Use your imagination to create personalized kits for birthdays or special events. Children enjoy participating by collecting and arranging items in various containers. Add fancy gift wrap and soon you can open your own boutique! A few kit ideas are:

- Preteens love beauty kits. Fill a wicker basket with fancy soaps, shampoos, and nail polish. Be practical and add a new toothbrush also. A few headbands or barrettes complete the kit.
- Encourage a child's love of reading with a book kit. Fill a canvas bag with bright bookmarks and a subscription to a new magazine. Add some new paperback books and a blank journal for the budding author to write his or her own novel.

- Every child enjoys a new set of crayons or felt pens. Check out art stores for markers that create wavy lines or double as stamps in various shapes. A package of fluorescent-colored paper displayed in a cardboard artist portfolio bag completes the art kit.
- Children love to build and take things apart. Why not assemble a "Fix-It" kit? A basic set of screwdrivers, wrenches, and a hammer stored in a small toolbox provides hours of fun. One mother included an old telephone for her daughter to take apart.
- With a little extra effort, dress-up kits can appeal to both boys and girls. Instead of simply putting fancy dresses in a box, make a few phone calls to locate actual uniforms. One mother obtained a doctor's smock, a firefighter's helmet, and a veterinarian lab coat to include in her nine year old's dress-up kit.

> For unique items to include in your kits, order the *Hearth Song Catalog.* They offer a recipe house kit, unusual dolls, and games. 1-800-325-2502.

Smell Those Cookies

What do you feel walking into a room filled with the aroma of fresh baked bread? What memories does the smell of Thanksgiving dinner evoke? Our sense of smell is another way God helps us appreciate our world.

If your house needs help overcoming a dirty-sock and wet-dog smell, maybe it's time to make a homemade potpourri. Sure you can buy potpourri in a variety of scents, but isn't it more fun to create your own as a family?

- The basic ingredient in potpourri is flowers. Roses, lavender, and sweet alyssum provide a wonderful fragrance. Ask a neighbor if you can collect loose petals from his or her flowers if you only have a few flowers. Our community has two display gardens with over fifty varieties of roses. We frequently visit and pick up the fallen petals to use in potpourri. After collecting petals, spread them on newspapers to dry. In several days, collect the dried petals and distribute them throughout the house.

- Display potpourri in distinctive containers like a large shell, teacup, or a miniature basket.

- Herbs from the garden create an earthier smell. Basil and rosemary combined with citrus peels and cinnamon produce a stronger, natural smell.

At a recent Bible study, a woman shared how her children loved to come home from school and smell homemade cookies. Since baking is at the bottom of my interest list, I developed a profound sense of guilt that my daughter was missing out on this childhood memory. Then it hit me. It was the smell of baking cookies that was important! I solved the problem by occasionally boiling a pot of water with cinnamon and vanilla. The house smells great, and the girls never miss the cookies!

Collect Those Whale Teeth

You've set out markers, made scented play dough, distributed board games, and still your children moan, "There's nothing to do!" One mother solved that problem by giving her children a list of chores to complete whenever they complained of boredom. They soon found ways to amuse themselves.

Sometimes trying a completely different type of craft beats the boredom blues. Carving scrimshaw provides children with a new experience with minimal mess.

In the nineteenth century, whalers developed the art of scrimshaw—carving on ivory, bones, or whale teeth. Your children don't need to get real whale's teeth to practice this ancient craft:

- Obtain some cone-shaped cups, the type found by water coolers.
- In an old bucket, mix 1 cup plaster of Paris and 1/2 cup water. Stir until mixture is smooth and the consistency of pudding. Add a few drops of water if the mixture is too thick.
- Pour plaster of Paris mixture into paper cones. Let set at least 24 hours.
- Remove the "teeth" from their paper molds. For best results, spray the plain teeth outdoors with Tuff Cote or Krylon Crystal Clear.
- Give your children a nail to scratch a design into the plaster of Paris tooth. Simple designs work best.
- Then rub a charcoal pencil or charcoal briquette into the carved design. Remove excess black smudges with a wet paper towel.

The finished product looks remarkably like authentic scrimshaw—at just a fraction of the cost. Keep several "whale teeth" handy for those times when your child needs help filling time.

Recipes You'll Never Want to Eat

Homemade Sparkles. Any art project can use sparkles. Instead of purchasing expensive glitter, try making your own. Stir five drops of food coloring into 1/2 cup salt. Mix well. Cook in microwave for approximately 1-1/2 to 2 minutes. Keep in a dry place and use as glitter.

- Colored Pasta. Ever wonder how to dye pasta bright colors for craft projects? Before you place the pasta in colored water, try this tip. Add three or four drops of food coloring to a cup of rubbing alcohol. Now add the pasta, stir, and drain. The alcohol transfers the color while retaining the hardness of pasta. Use for stringing necklaces, decorating jewelry boxes, or making colorful collages. This also works to color rice.

- Slurpch. Kids and adults love handling this unique substance. In a paper cup or empty can, mix 1/2 cup white glue and 1/4 cup liquid starch. Stir. Watch the glue and starch change to a new consistency ideal to stretch, roll, and shape. Store in a self-sealing plastic bag.

- Sweet-Smelling Craft Dough. To make great-smelling craft dough for a variety of projects, follow these simple directions. Mix 1 cup sifted flour, 3 tablespoons oil, and 1/2 cup salt. Stir in any flavor of unsweetened powdered drink mix. With adult supervision, add 1 cup boiling water and stir. Knead until mixture turns into a soft dough.

- Beads Galore. Mix 1 cup salt and 1/2 cup cornstarch in a saucepan. With adult supervision, add 1/2 cup boiling water and stir well. Add a few drops of food color and keep mixture over low heat for 3-4 minutes. Remove from heat and allow to cool. Roll dough into small beads. Use a toothpick to form a hole in the center. Let dry overnight. Paint beads and create your own jewelry.

More Recipes You'll Never Want to Eat

While preschoolers eagerly dive into a batch of home-made play dough with their hands, older children like to create detailed objects. The following white bread dough recipe is ideal for intricate projects. The dough is a pliable, elastic mixture that resists cracking.

- Rip one or two slices of white bread (crusts removed) into small pieces. Place in a bowl and add 1 tablespoon of white glue. Mix with a fork until it is a smooth, gummy consistency. If it feels too sticky, add a few more pieces of torn bread. Create your sculpture. Let it air dry from one to three days depending on your climate.

- Scented Doughs: When mixing any play dough recipe, add your own scents. A sprinkle of cinnamon or peppermint extract adds a pleasant aroma while creating objects. Take one mother's advice though—"Garlic-powdered play dough is not a pleasant sensory experience!"

- All-Purpose Play Clay: Mix 1 cup flour, 1 cup water, 1/2 cup salt, 1 teaspoon vegetable oil, and 1/2 teaspoon cream of tartar in a saucepan. (A few drops food color are optional.) Cook over medium heat until the mixture sticks together in a big clump. Drop onto a floured kitchen counter and allow to cool before children handle. Knead from four to five minutes and then use as you would any regular play dough. The mixture air dries in several days, or use over and over by storing in an airtight container.

- Smelly Ornaments (good smelly, that is!): Mix 1 cup applesauce, 1-1/2 cups cinnamon, 1/3 cup glue to form a ball. Chill at least thirty minutes. Roll dough to 1/4 inch thickness. (If too thin, designs crack.) Cut out dough using cookie cutters. Use a straw to punch a hole in the top for hanging. Let dry at room temperature for two days. Makes about 25 average size "cookies."

The Incredible Clay Book by Sherry Haah and Laura Torres, Klutz Press. This eighty-four-page book provides ideas and clear instructions. It even comes with eight blocks of clay.

Gyotaku

Boutiques and art galleries sell them for a large amount of money. Now you have a chance to create your own gyotaku at a fraction of the cost.

Gyotaku, or Japanese fish printing, has been used for over one hundred years to record the size and characteristics of fish.

To make your own fish print, the first and most obvious step is to obtain a fish. You'll need a fresh one, usually available at any grocery store. Pat excess moisture off the fish. Be careful not to rub off the scales. Stuff the fish with tissue paper to create a firmer surface. Give plastic gloves to family members squeamish about touching a dead fish. Set out several colors of tempera paint, and you're ready to begin. Brush the paint over the fish. It's up to you if you want to stick with one color or use several to distinguish the head or eyes.

When the fish is covered with paint, carefully place a piece of butcher paper on top. Press down on the paper, making contact with the entire fish. Smooth gently over the fins, gills, and body. Remove the paper to reveal a reverse print of the fish. Experiment with the amount of paint to use on the fish. Your family can make several prints to get one they like. We've used one fish for more than twenty-five prints. Let the paint dry and display proudly.

In addition to making a picture, fish prints can be used in other ways:

- A large sheet of butcher paper turns into wrapping paper with numerous fish prints on it.
- Use fabric paint to create a fish print on a T-shirt.
- Smaller fish prints, such as trout, make great designs on personalized lunch bags.

Gyotaku Fish Impressions: The Art of Fish Impressions by Doug Olander and Frank Amato. Published by Frank Amato Publications, 1994. Publication is an oversized book with extensive related information.

All Wrapped Up

If homemade gifts require too much time and effort, have children make homemade wrapping paper instead. Recipients appreciate the special touch of a gift covered in custom-designed paper.

- Take plain, brown grocery bags and turn them inside out if they have writing on them. Use a paper punch to punch holes about two inches apart at the top. Decorate the bag with stickers, stencils, or paint. Place a gift inside and weave a colorful ribbon in and out of the punched holes to close the bag.

- Place a large sheet of plain wrapping paper on a flat surface. If you're feeling brave, have your children dip their hands in paint and make designs on the paper. Add interest by using painted feet on the paper.

- Tear pieces of colored crepe paper and place on a large sheet of plain, colored paper. Take a spray bottle and gently "mist" the crepe paper. The color bleeds off, making a colorful abstract design on the wrapping paper. Carefully lift and discard the wet crepe paper.

- Wrap a gift in plain-colored wrapping paper. Use cookie cutters to trace shapes on aluminum foil. Cut out the designs and glue them on the box to make a shiny gift box.

- Take the same cookie cutters and dip them in paint to use in decorating plain wrapping paper.

- Place the gift in a box and wrap it with paper. Take a piece of thick, colored yarn and dip it in glue. Wipe off the excess glue and wrap yarn around the box in various shapes and patterns. Let it dry and present your spider web boxed gift.

- Crumple white paper into a loose ball and dip it into a bowl of tea. Unroll the tea-dyed paper and let dry. The stain and wrinkles give the paper an antique look.

The Common Crayon

OK, what can you do with a box of ordinary crayons? They're probably scattered all over your house behind furniture and in the deep recesses of drawers. Dig them out, gather the family together, and see what you can do with the ever-popular crayon.

• Try painting with melted crayon. You won't be able to do detailed work, but any drawing with a bold design works. Peel the wrappers off all your broken crayons. (For easier peeling, soak crayons in a tub of cool water overnight, then peel off labels.) Place crayons in a double boiler (adults only) until they begin melting. Remove from the heat and use wooden sticks or old paintbrushes to paint.

• Place a piece of waxed paper on a work surface. Use a cheese grater to shave peeled crayons onto waxed paper. Cover with another sheet of waxed paper and iron slowly on low heat until the crayons melt. Trim excess waxed paper and hang your sun-catcher in a window.

• Make a clean crayon carving by mixing four tablespoons of hand soap, cut into tiny pieces. Place in a pan and heat with three tablespoons of water. Add crayon shavings—two to three tablespoons of any color. Continue stirring until mixture melts. Fill yogurt containers 1/2 full with mixture and/or shape into balls. Let dry at least forty-eight hours and you have a clean carving medium.

• Collect all your peeled, broken crayon stubs and place them in a double boiler. Melt slowly and pour the mixture into an old muffin pan. Try sorting crayons by color, or experiment to see what happens when you mix various colors together. After wax hardens, you'll have giant multi-colored crayons.

• Give your child a piece of paper cut from a paper grocery bag. Draw a picture using strong pressure and deep colors. Crumple the paper, unroll, and crumple again several times. Smooth out the paper and paint over the design with watercolors. The crayon resists paint and fills in the paper cracks, making a batik effect.

Wild and Wonderful Windows

Every imaginable holiday offers the chance to purchase paraphernalia—cardboard shamrocks, plastic hearts, and inflatable snowmen. But rather than purchase all this stuff, and to save on costs while increasing your children's creativity, allow them to paint decorations on your windows for specific holidays. Yes, it might get messy, so be sure to tape around the edge of the window pane to avoid getting paint on the window trim. Old towels or newspaper on the floor make clean-up easier. One mother, who regularly lets her children paint the living room window, gives them small brushes and cotton swabs. This cuts down on the drips and mess of using large paint brushes.

Painting free-form on the window works fine, but for better results, try this technique:

- Lay out butcher paper the size of your window.
- Have children outline their pictures directly on the paper. This gives them freedom to erase or add details to their artwork.
- When everyone is satisfied with the design, tape it to the outside of the window.
- Children can now "trace" and paint their picture from the inside.
- To make clean-up easier, add a few drops of clear, dishwashing soap to the liquid tempera paint.

As a get-acquainted activity, a Sunday school teacher let her students decorate their classroom windows at the beginning of the year. Another family used their French door with individual glass panes as an activity for their annual Fourth of July party. Guests dressed in casual summer clothes got to select a small pane and decorate it with red, white, and blue paint.